IN THE IMAGE OF GOD

IN THE IMAGE OF GOD

by
Michael Edgecombe

with contributions by
Rebecca Lines and Russell Taylor

The Christadelphian
404 Shaftmoor Lane
Hall Green
Birmingham B28 8SZ, UK

2011

First published 2011

ISBN 978-085189186-6

Printed and bound in Malta by:
GUTENBERG PRESS LIMITED

CONTENTS

Where chapters are focused on specific passages of
Scripture, these have been listed to facilitate access.

vi

PREFACE

THIS book sets out to review Scripture's consistent teaching on man and woman in the purpose of God, beginning in Genesis, and concluding in Revelation – the order in which God has chosen to reveal Himself, His Son and His will for us.

The book developed from a series of articles under the same title, which ran in *The Christadelphian* from January 2008 to May 2009. The series was co-authored with Sister Rebecca Lines and Brother Russell Taylor, and the author records his gratitude and thanks for their significant contribution, as also for the work of many other brothers and sisters who have thought and written on this subject. He takes full responsibility for the present text, however.

The subject is a sensitive one for brothers and sisters, who must understand and apply the teaching and practice of the Lord Jesus and his apostles, against the background of the law and the prophets, in an age that considers them ignorant and bigoted, and dismisses the authority of the Bible for the individual, the family, and the people of God. If, however, we enter into the spirit of the Lord and his apostles, interpret their teaching accurately, "rightly handling the Word of truth", and apply it faithfully, "speaking the truth in love", we cannot go too far wrong.

The fact that we are out of step with Western society is awkward, but hardly surprising. The gospel of the cross, God's blunt challenge to human notions of power and wisdom, is as counter-cultural today as it was in Corinth about AD 50. The twenty-first century ecclesia must build on the first century foundation of the apostles and prophets, "Jesus Christ himself being the chief cornerstone". "Upon this rock" the Lord is building his ecclesia. If we build, we build with him: and he will prevail.

The author is conscious that he writes as a male. Every word has been laid down with enormous respect for the important women in his life – above all his wife and his daughter, but also his mother, sisters, grandmother, mother-in-law, sisters-in-law, cousins, nieces, friends and sisters in the family of God – much too many to name. He has endeavoured wholeheartedly to 'give honour' to them, as God has asked all men to do, and he apologises in advance for any clumsiness or hurt, which he does not intend.

MICHAEL EDGECOMBE
2011

1

UNCHANGING TRUTHS IN A CHANGING SOCIETY

THERE are few relationships more important than that between man and woman; and few more challenging, as every book of quotations testifies by its columns of cynical wit. The relationship is unique among created things. The animals, male and female, were conjured independently from the sea, the air, the ground; and prolific life broke out everywhere. For us it was different. One man was shaped by God from the clay: one woman was formed around man's rib, again by God.

A vital relationship

We are two complete but complementary beings, able to live independently of each other, but drawn magnetically together: because God's intention has always been that in marriage, in family life, in the ecclesia, in the workplace and in the community – on every hill and in every valley of life – we might together co-create something greater than either of us, bigger than both, more than the sum of the parts. Yet our relationship, whether married or single, is not an easy one: and from Genesis to Revelation the Spirit acknowledges the difficulties and complexities and disappointments and failings that so often affect us, as also it celebrates notable examples of secure, happy, fruitful, God-honouring man–woman relationships.

Perhaps the most powerful testimony to the significance of our relationship is from the pen of Paul, who wrote to the brothers and sisters of Ephesus about the relationship between wife and husband: yet ultimately about something more than marriage, for, he

1

said, "This mystery is profound, and I am saying that it refers to Christ and the church" (Ephesians 5:32).

So we cannot allow ourselves to slide into disappointed bitterness or world-weary cynicism when we think and speak about the relationship between man and woman. We have been joined to Christ. So we must try to come at the topic from God's perspective: to see with fresh eyes the lovely ideal shaped in dewy Eden; to lament the alienating effects of sin and the sadness and pain it has inflicted on woman and man; to rejoice in the new hope brought to so many by the obedience of the Son; to live and work in faith, and hope, and love, "looking to Jesus, the founder and perfecter of our faith"; to press forward to the day when those who have accepted the invitation of the Spirit and the Bride can be joined inseparably to the Lamb, return to the Garden, and eat together from the Tree of Life. This is the way in which God, and His Son, and His servants, have asked us to think and speak and write about the relationship between man and woman.

And that is what we wish to do. For the subject has become a pressing one. The question has been put to God's family by a number in recent years: What is the Bible's teaching about man and woman? What did God intend when He created man and woman in the beginning? How are we to interpret the consequences of sin? What principles have guided godly men and women through the centuries? How did the death and resurrection of the Lord Jesus make a difference to the man–woman relationship? What did the apostles "command and teach"? And how is their instruction to be interpreted and applied today?

Society's attitude

For society, of course, this question is of little interest. It has long since decided what its attitude will be, and it has no regard for the Bible as the living Word of the living God.

Western society has moved steadily toward a broadly-based equality, at least in principle, a trend grounded in the humanist philosophy of the Enlightenment, and expressed eloquently in the opening words of the Constitution of the United States of America, adopted in 1787: "We hold these truths to be self-evident, that all men are created equal." Self-evident? Philosophers still argue whether human equality is self-evident, but the doctrine was sincerely believed.

Hot on the heels of American independence came the French Revolution of 1789, out of which the motto "Liberté, égalité, fraternité!" emerged. The social upheaval of the Revolution, widespread improvements in education, health and working conditions, the emergence of free markets and the labour movement have created political, social and religious freedoms that have benefited men and women, black and white, the downtrodden and the poor all over the world.

The rights movement gained new impetus in the years after World War II, with a series of declarations on human rights by the United Nations, beginning with the *Universal Declaration of Human Rights* in 1948, and the civil rights movement brought about wide-ranging social reforms through the 1960s and 1970s.

The movement for the rights of women has been an important thread in this story. The campaign for women's suffrage slowly gained ground through the nineteenth century, and catalysed a major change in social attitudes in the years around World War I, establishing legal rights for women such as the right to vote and the right to hold property.

French feminist Simone de Beauvoir published *The Second Sex* in 1949, but it was some time before a second wave of feminism swept the Western world in the 1960s and 1970s, led by such forceful advocates as Betty Friedan (*The Feminine Mystique*, 1963), Germaine Greer (*The Female Eunuch*, 1970) and Gloria Steinem (*Ms* magazine, 1972). This second wave aimed to establish legislated rights for recognition and status; equal access to education, health services and credit;

family rights, including no fault divorce; affirmative action on employment, pay, conditions and career progress; admission to the military and judiciary; and reproduction, including access to contraception and the right to abort an unborn child. The rights movement continues today.

The response of the church

Changes in society have reverberated in the church: and most Christian churches have revised many of their traditional positions.

Most advocates of change have argued simply that the church must listen to society, must reflect changing community norms in order to remain credible and relevant. Others, however, particularly in evangelical churches, have made their case not from society but from the Bible. They have argued that the Bible has been misinterpreted; that the exclusion of women from leadership and teaching roles reflects a patriarchal bias in the church; that God, the Lord Jesus and the apostles always intended that women should fulfil these roles alongside men, without distinction.

Adopting these views, many churches – most synods of the Evangelical or Lutheran Church, some communions of the Anglican Church, the Methodist Church, the Uniting Church and many charismatic churches – have inducted women into the clergy. Some have taken the logic of equality further still and inducted practicing homosexuals, men and women, into the ministry.

What does the Bible really say? Are the churches right? Should we follow them?

2

AN IMPORTANT QUESTION

AGAINST the backdrop of these changes it is interesting and instructive to note a number of statements by our early brothers.

Although John Thomas was highly appreciative of women, and cared deeply about his invalid wife and his daughter, he was scathing about moves for suffrage in his days, and said as much in *Elpis Israel*. It is fair to observe that Queen Victoria, one of the most powerful women of her day, felt just as strongly. In a letter to Prince Albert's biographer, she wrote:

> "The Queen is most anxious to enlist everyone who can speak or write to join in checking this mad, wicked folly of 'Woman's Rights', with all its attendant horrors, on which her poor feeble sex is bent, forgetting every sense of womanly feeling and propriety ... It is a subject that makes the Queen so furious that she cannot contain herself. God created men and women different – then let them remain each in their own position ... Woman would become the most hateful, heartless and disgusting of human beings were she allowed to unsex herself."*

Early statements

John Thomas' statements should be read against the backdrop of views held widely by leading women and men in his day: and not judged unreasonably. Taken as a whole they indicate a high view of women, but strong opposition to their involvement in politics, public speaking and leadership roles, based not on personal prejudices but on his reading of the Bible. We refer to

---

* L Strachey, *Queen Victoria* (New York: Harcourt, Brace & Co, 1921): 409.

them only because they have sometimes been used in an unfair attempt to dismiss his exposition.

From the platform in Birmingham in 1874, Robert Roberts protested heatedly against the denigration of women:

"I have heard some speak contemptuously of the sisters as 'mere women, only fit to nurse babies, and look after the pudding'. Against such a doctrine, every true brother will earnestly protest. It is not only degrading to her whom God has given us for 'an helpmeet', but it is inconsistent with the spirit of the gospel which teaches that there is neither male nor female in Christ: that we are *all one in Christ Jesus* ... Sisters are never likely to develop into noble servants of Christ if the door is shut in their face, by a theory which would consign them to cradles, pots and pans ... to insist on confining sisters to these, would be to ignore the fact that they have brains as well as bodies; and that men have other needs of help-meetship, besides those of knife and fork. Such a boorish doctrine would destroy companionship, where brethren need it most, and unfit their wives to fulfil the highest function of motherhood, which is to bring up their children in the nurture and admonition of the Lord. In fact it is a doctrine to be opposed and detested as much as any hurtful doctrine may be. The man who holds, and much more the man who preaches it, deserves to be deprived of every social advantage and be shut up in a cave. This in fact, is his destiny at last."*

He maintained this attitude consistently to the end of his life. Addressing a question that had divided an ecclesia about whether the advice of sisters should be sought and listened to in "the non-public working or management of things", he observed:

---

* "Sunday morning at the Christadelphian Synagogue, Birmingham", No. 56, *The Christadelphian* 11(7) (July 1874): 312. The emphasis is original.

"You can no more suppress a wise woman's influence and a wise woman's voice than you can suppress the law of gravitation. You may prevent her delivering a public address: but you cannot prevent her giving good counsel, and you ought not. Though woman by divine law is in subjection, she is not to be extinguished ... I have seen tyrannical and unsympathetic men wrongly using Paul's authority to put down and quench godly women more qualified than they themselves to exercise judgment and give counsel. Let women certainly be modest, but let her not be reduced to a cypher, which God never intended ... We ought to be thankful when women turn up who are able to help with wise suggestion."*

Robert Roberts' views were no idle theory. Jane Roberts was a woman of great character who was highly valued by her husband as a fellow-worker in daily life and service for Christ, strongly influencing his thinking and practice.

Christadelphian practice

We have quoted these statements at some length not because they are authoritative, but because they contrast with social attitudes widespread in the nineteenth century. Many men considered women second-rate citizens, confined them to domestic minutiae, denigrated their conversation and discounted their opinions. God forbid that such attitudes should be found within the four walls of His family! They are certainly no part of our heritage.

For Christadelphians, being avid readers of the word of God, thought differently. Values, beliefs and practices as individual disciples, as ecclesias, as the family of God, were to be decided by the Bible, not dictated by community attitudes – in the matter of male and female roles, as in other aspects of faith and practice. Believers understood that men and women – brothers and sisters

---

* "A voyage to Australia, New Zealand, and other lands", *The Christadelphian* 34(2) (February 1897): 60.

in Christ – were of equal value in the sight of God, and spiritual partners, not only in this life, but in the coming kingdom.

The higher status of Christadelphian women was reflected in ecclesial arrangements. The gospel was carried by women as well as men, to women as well as men. Sisters had an equal vote with brothers from the earliest constitutions. They were encouraged to write for *The Christadelphian* magazine on a range of topics, and their suggestions on prophecy or expositional questions were treated with the utmost respect. Their status as "joint heirs of the grace of life" equally with brothers was acknowledged.

At the same time, some distinctions were made. Brothers were members of arranging committees: sisters were not. Brothers chaired public meetings, and spoke from the platform: sisters did not. A balance was struck between spiritual equality for brothers and sisters, and distinctive, complementary roles in the ecclesia and the home. Most ecclesias have maintained these distinctions to the present day. Whether they are valid, or not, is something we shall examine.

An important question that will not go away

One thing we cannot say is that this matter is unimportant. Paul, "the apostle of Jesus Christ to the Gentiles", states that it was among the apostolic traditions or ordinances delivered to ecclesias for their compliance (1 Corinthians 11:2). The practice he taught was the common teaching of all the apostles and the common practice of all the ecclesias of God (verse 16; 14:33,34). His teachings were, in fact, "the commandments of the Lord", and he insisted that they be acknowledged as such (verse 37). The detail of his instruction was part of a general requirement that ecclesias operate decently and in order (verse 40), springing from God's inherent love of order (verse 33). He regarded breaches of this teaching as shameful and dishonouring (11:2-16; 14:33-35), he would not permit any other practice (1 Timothy 2:12), and he refused to recognise those who would not accept what he had said (1 Corinthians 14:38). We might not have included Paul's teaching about this subject on our list of fundamentals, but in the light of these statements we cannot consider it unimportant, a matter of personal preference and general indifference.

Many who prefer traditional approaches, and believe them to be self-evidently Biblical, might consider the case open and shut, and hope that the question will simply go away. The evidence from other denominations is that it will not. Professor Wayne Grudem, a Southern Baptist who has been studying these developments across denominations since the 1980s, concludes:

"The controversy will not go away until it has been resolved by the vast majority of evangelical groups and denominations. The pressures in the culture are so great that no church and no denomination and no parachurch organization can simply decide to avoid the controversy. Each group that has not done so will have to study this issue and reach a formal position on it."*

Our approach

The only responsible course, therefore, is to open up these questions together, and to search together for sound, Biblical answers. And that is the counsel of the apostles: "Test everything; hold fast what is good" (1 Thessalonians 5:21). We have nothing to lose and everything to gain from "receiving the word with all eagerness, examining the Scriptures".

Our aim is to arrive at answers that are neither conservative nor progressive, neither traditional nor radical, neither old nor new, but Biblical: for we can only be changed into the glory of the Lord and experience the true freedom which belongs to His children if we listen to, reflect on and obey the new and old, living and life-giving voice of God.

---

* W Grudem, *Countering the Claims of Evangelical Feminism: Biblical Responses to the Key Questions* (Multnomah, 2006): 302-303.

3

"MALE AND FEMALE HE CREATED THEM"

WE shall begin at the beginning, and follow the story as God has told it; which brings us to the sixth day. While the world had been filled with abundant, teeming life by the Spirit of God, there was something missing. What He had created was good, but not *very* good.

In the image and likeness of God
In the council of heaven God spoke again:

"'Let us make man in our image, after our likeness. And let them have dominion ...'
So God created man in his own image, in the image of God he created him; male and female he created them. And God blessed them. And God said to them, 'Be fruitful and multiply and fill the earth and subdue it and have dominion ...'" (Genesis 1:26-28)

This crowning act is the only creative act preceded by an inclusive word to the angels. It is narrated at greater length. And while before it everything was "good", once it had been completed the whole creation was "very good" (1:31).

The record makes five notable points. First, God was personally involved. On the fifth day God had said, "Let the waters bring forth". On the sixth day He had said, "Let the earth bring forth". But now God said, "Let *us* make". God would be personally involved in the creation of man and woman, because on them He would bestow all His most precious gifts. Man was shaped by the power of God: and the Lord God Himself bent down to breathe life into his nostrils. Woman in turn was shaped by the Lord God around the man's rib. Neither

10

simply emerged from the sea or the earth by the authority of His voice, as the animals had done.

Second, man was to be made in the image and likeness of God: or, as Paul interprets the statement, "in the image and glory of God". Man was intended to be as close a representation of the uncreate God as a created thing could be. Like God, man was to be self-aware, to have a sense of identity and self-concept, to think, to speak and to act, to love and to hate, to rejoice and to grieve, to create and to destroy. Alone among created beings man can know and love God, understand and believe His word, understand His ways, enjoy a relationship with Him, manifest His character, do His will, contribute to His purpose. Man is wonderful insofar as man is like God, and fulfils the destiny dreamed for man by God. Move away from this likeness, and man becomes more and more "like the beasts that perish" (Psalm 49:12,20).

Although this likeness has been degraded by the Fall and its aftermath, we continue to be "God's offspring" (Acts 17:29), "made in the likeness of God" (James 3:9) and therefore "the image and glory of God" (1 Corinthians 11:7). We are destined "to be conformed to the image of his Son" (Romans 8:29), who is "the image of the invisible God" (Colossians 1:15; 2 Corinthians 4:4), so that "when he appears we shall be like him" (1 John 3:2). God is at work by His Spirit to accomplish this change "from one degree of glory to another" (2 Corinthians 3:18), even now, as we "put off ... the old self" and "put on the new self", our minds being "renewed in knowledge after the image of its creator" (Colossians 3:10; Ephesians 4:22-24). He will perfect His work when at the Lord's return we shall be changed in a moment from "the image of the man of dust" to the much more glorious "image of the man of heaven" (1 Corinthians 15:49).

One being in two halves

Third, man was a "them", one being in two complementary halves. Earlier acts of creation had

11

already seen sea creatures and birds, wild beasts, domestic stock and "creeping things" created male and female. But from the beginning God conceived man as a "them", male and female together, unique among created things in being made after the pattern of His own image and likeness. Forever after, man and woman would stand before God, equally His creatures.

Fourth, the "them" was to "have dominion" or "rule over" the whole creation. Hence David marvelled at man's situation. Such a small and helpless thing under the great stretch of shining sky! So insignificant among the great spheres that wheel through the universe about him! Yet what an extraordinary weight of glory God has conferred on this creature, little less than the angels, crowned with glory and honour, handed the dominion over all the works spun from His hands, all things subjected to him! By "dominion" God does not have in mind the oppressive, autocratic rule that has been exercised by most kings down through history, doing their own will for their own advantage and glory. Rather, man was to rule as God's deputy, doing God's will for the benefit of God's creation and the glory of God's name.

All this true of man, "male and female"! "O LORD, our Lord, how majestic is your name in all the earth!" (Psalm 8:9; cp. 72:8).

A shared blessing

Finally, God blessed man. A human blessing may come to nothing; but this blessing was spoken by God, Whose words create and give life, Who speaks and it is done. The blessing of God "guarantees and effects the hoped for success"*. As the man and the woman embraced the will of God for their life together and recognized and rejoiced in their complementary identities as male and female, they would find fulfillment in the purpose for which they were created. They would be blessed, becoming "fruitful and multiplying", having children

---

* G Wenham, *Genesis,* Word Biblical Commentary (Waco: Word Books, 1987): 24.

and raising a family together, exercising God's dominion over the Creation together.

So Genesis 1, with its cosmic sweep, concludes with the creation and blessing of man, male and female:

"And on the seventh day God ended his work that he had done, and he rested on the seventh day." (2:2)

4

"I WILL MAKE HIM A HELPER"

THE first creation record is followed by a second, detailed account of the creation of the man and the woman, and their union in the garden of God. The accounts are different but complementary – somewhat like man and woman themselves. Genesis 1 emphasises the equality of the man and the woman. Both bear the image and likeness of God. They are equally God's creation, equally His children, in His image and likeness, equally central to His purpose, equally destined to have dominion, equally blessed. But differences emerge in Genesis 2 – differences that are important.

"It is not good that the man should be alone"

For a time Adam was alone. He was placed in the garden, commissioned to steward the garden, and given a law forbidding him to eat of "the tree of the knowledge of good and evil". His first task seems to have been the naming of the animals as they were brought to him by God, a first expression of the responsible dominion intended by his Maker from the beginning (1:28).

But the process was set up by God for an even deeper purpose, and it is introduced by His own observation: "It is not good that the man should be alone" (2:18). It is obvious that He did not suddenly conceive woman as an afterthought. God knew full well that His creation could not be "very good" while the male continued alone and incomplete. But it was crucial that Adam, and all men after him, should see things in the same clear light. Man was never to think of himself as independent, self-complete and self-sufficient. Woman was never to be thought of by man as merely a convenient appendage, created to make life easier for him. She was to be the essential companion.

So God deliberately structured the process of creation to teach this lesson: and Adam learned it well. Man was created solitary, and left solitary for a time until he himself felt the need for a mate. Perhaps God even mentioned it to him. The words, "for Adam there was not found a helper" (2:20), may suggest a conscious search on his part. Be that as it may, as the animals passed before him, it came home to Adam powerfully that he was, unlike them, alone; lonely, in fact; longing for and in great need of a companion.

"A help meet for him"

Thus God resolved, "I will make him a helper fit for him". The phrase "help meet for him" (KJV) is a translation of two Hebrew words, *êzer*, 'help' and *neged*, here acting as a preposition meaning 'before', 'facing' or 'in the presence of'.

Commentators have debated whether "help" inherently refers to a lesser role. The term is sometimes used of those superior in authority and strength, sometimes of those equal, and sometimes of those lesser. Indeed, it is mostly used in the Hebrew Scriptures of God Himself (e.g., Psalm 33:20; 70:5; 115:9; 121:2). In every case, however – including those cases in which God is the helper – the person or persons being helped have a primary responsibility, and the person or persons providing the help are assisting them to fulfil that responsibility.

In Adam's case, he had primary responsibility for the work God had given him – the tending of God's garden and the keeping of God's law. That God did in fact hold the man primarily responsible is evident in the very next chapter. The woman was created by God to help the man in those tasks. She was to be always with him, by his side, in his presence, so that they should together carry forward God's work. Without her, Adam was inadequate: together, they could fulfil the great destiny God had mapped out for them.

"This at last"

Was Adam told he was being put into a deep sleep, and why? Did he knowingly cooperate with God? These events point forward to the Lord Jesus' own sacrifice, as he voluntarily yielded his body and submitted to a deep sleep that his Bride might be created from his wounded side (John 19:34) – a spiritual woman built around his body and blood.

As consciousness had first come to Adam, as "God breathed into his nostrils the breath of life", and the inert clay form stirred, he found himself gazing into the eyes of God. As he now returned to consciousness, his eyes met those of Eve, the last and the loveliest of God's creatures, created from his side, deliberately establishing an intimate psychological, emotional and spiritual bond.

Never can there have been a man and a woman so perfect for each other; and Adam's heart went out to her at once. His great longing was fulfilled (2:23):

"This at last is bone of my bones,
and flesh of my flesh;
She shall be called Woman,
because she was taken out of Man".

Adam highly prized the companion God presented to him; and, says Paul, "in the same way husbands should love their wives as their own bodies" (Ephesians 5:28). God pronounced them husband and wife, joining them in marriage (Matthew 19:5); and at last His creation was blissfully complete, and "very good".

A careful balance

What can we say about the relationship between the man and the woman at this point? A careful balance is evident in the two complementary accounts of creation. In the first we have man, one being in two halves, man male and female. No difference is made. The man and the woman are both specially created by God, both in His image and likeness, both to have dominion, both blessed by Him. In their significance to God, in their

16

spiritual capacity, and in their destiny, male and female were conceived by God from the beginning as equals.

In the second, more detailed account, additional facts are revealed. We are told that the man was made first, the woman second. We are told that the woman was made from the man. We are told that the woman was created to fulfil a deep need experienced by the man. We are told that the woman was an essential companion for the man, and that without her he was fundamentally incomplete, and knew it.

Creation facts

The apostle comes back to these truths in the first century: and upon them, and the reality to which they point in Jesus Christ, he builds a coherent understanding of the relationship between male and female in the home and in the ecclesia.

First, there was an order: the man, then the woman. So Paul reminds us: "Adam was formed first, then Eve" (1 Timothy 2:13). God created the woman after the man. Second, says Paul, "Man was not made from woman, but woman from man" (1 Corinthians 11:8). This is highlighted by Adam's own joyful poetry, "She shall be called Woman, because she was taken out of Man". God created the woman out of the man. Third, says Paul, "Neither was man created for woman, but woman for man" (verse 9). God created the woman to help the man.

After the man; from the man; to help the man. These Creation facts are important in Paul's teaching, as we shall see. For now, we simply note them.

Paul hastens to add, lest men should egotistically distort these facts, "Nevertheless, in the Lord woman is not independent of man nor man of woman" (verse 11). Just as they were designed to be perfect companions in marriage, so they are to be perfect companions in the ecclesia. Even "in the Lord" male and female are incomplete without each other.

17

And, he continues, "For as woman was made from man, so man is now born of woman" (verse 12). It may be true that the female originated from the male, but it is also true that a man's natural existence can only come about through the long period during which the woman bears the developing embryo, shielding and nurturing the fragile new life with her own body. And even at a spiritual level these things are true: for while the ecclesia owes its very existence to the Lord Jesus, he in turn owes his existence, in part, to the obedience and care of a young woman who yielded her body, before his conception, to the will of God.

But any to and fro argument is cut off with a firm full stop: "And all things are of God". And that is that. God is our Creator and Lifegiver, our Provider and Redeemer. "The LORD, he is God! It is he who made us, and we are his" (Psalm 100:3). We must never forget who has made us, and whose we are. Remembering this fundamental fact puts everything into perspective.

5

"SIN CAME INTO THE WORLD
THROUGH ONE MAN"

A T the end of Genesis 2 we are still in the world's golden dawn, where the man and the woman spend their days working together in the garden, and enjoy in the evenings a pure and lovely fellowship with God.

'The woman, being deceived'

We do not know how long this delightful tranquility lasted, but at some point the serpent, "more crafty" or "more subtil" (KJV) than any other animal, offered Eve a different set of spectacles, an alternative way to understand the law God had given to the man.

It was a divine conspiracy, the serpent suggested. The law was not authoritative. The negative outcome which God had warned of – death – was not sure and certain. Actually, the law was unreasonable and elitist, designed rather selfishly to keep the man and the woman in their place, "a little lower than the angels" in God's hierarchy. He implied that it was in their best interests to break the law. There were blessings to be had: new experiences, new insights, new status, new knowledge, bringing moral autonomy and self-determination. It was all theirs for the taking.

Eve was already "like God": for she had been made, with Adam, in the image and likeness of God (1:27). The garden was full of lovely sights and delicious foods: for every tree was "pleasant to the sight and good for food" (2:9). She had access to the knowledge of good and evil through daily contact with God in the garden, and she was growing in wisdom every day.

But the serpent's plausible lies stirred in her a complex of lusts for the one thing she should not have –

19

the fruit of the tree of the knowledge of good and evil. Strong new desires changed the way she thought: the lust of the flesh, the lust of the eyes, "the boasting of what [a man] has and does" (1 John 2:16, NIV). "The woman was deceived and became a transgressor" (1 Timothy 2:14). She could no longer see things as God had taught her to see them. The serpent was right! She must act to address this injustice, seize this opportunity, and secure her destiny. She reached out, she took the fruit, and she ate it. She passed it to her husband, and he, too, ate it.

The silence of Adam

Was Adam with Eve in the crisis of temptation? He was certainly present at the moment she yielded to it: "She also gave some to her husband who was with her" (Genesis 3:6). It was to Adam that God delivered express moral instructions concerning the trees of the garden (2:16,17). Yet at no point did Eve seek her husband's counsel. Even more critically, Adam was deathly silent. God's first words in rebuking him were, "Because you have listened to the voice of your wife" (3:17). When the word of God with which he had been entrusted was being challenged, when his wife's faith in God was being undermined, he failed to speak out or act in defence of God's word – or of his wife.

Hence the apostle Paul writes, "As in Adam all die" (1 Corinthians 15:22,45-49); and painstakingly attributes to Adam the introduction of sin and death:

"Sin came into the world through one man, and death through sin ... many died through one man's trespass ... because of one man's trespass, death reigned ... as one trespass led to condemnation for all men ... as by the one man's disobedience the many were made sinners."   (Romans 5:12-21)

For this reason also, it was Adam whom God first summoned to account (Genesis 3:9); and it was due to Adam specifically that the ground was cursed (3:17).

It is interesting to observe the reversal of order that arrives with Genesis 3. The record of Genesis 1 and 2 consistently demonstrates the God-appointed order of Eden through phrases such as "male and female", "taken out of man", "brought her to the man", "bone of my bones and flesh of my flesh", "the man and his wife" (1:27; 2:22,23,25). But this order is reversed early in Genesis 3 with the words "she took of its fruit and ate, and she also gave some to her husband who was with her; and he ate" (3:6).* Adam and Eve, secure and blessed in Eden, could not possibly have anticipated the outcome for all mankind of this first, tragic instance of role-reversal.

Creation corrupted

The moment of judgement came, as it must. The serpent was cursed above all other beasts, sentenced to crawl forever through the dying, dusty world he had corrupted by his lies. Cursing, degradation, enmity, pain, frustration, toil, death and dissolution – this was his legacy.

The ground, too, would be cursed, and Adam would suffer. But first God turned to Eve:

"I will surely multiply your pain in childbearing;
in pain you shall bring forth children.

Your desire shall be for your husband,
and he shall rule over you" (Genesis 3:16)

The human pair had been blessed with the words, "Be fruitful and multiply and fill the earth" (1:28). But now their blessing could be experienced only through toilsome labour and multiplied pain.

These changes, unwelcome in themselves, are nevertheless interpreted by Paul as having a purpose that is ultimately positive. With respect to Adam, Paul writes:

"The creation was subjected to futility, not willingly, but because of him who subjected it, in hope

---

* This order is immediately restored following God's intervention and ruling – "The man called his wife's name Eve"; "for Adam and for his wife"; "sent him out"; "drove out the man"; "Adam knew Eve his wife"; "Adam knew his wife again"; "male and female" (3:20,21,23,24; 4:1,25; 5:2, etc.).

that the creation itself will be set free from its bondage to decay and obtain the freedom of the glory of the children of God." (Romans 8:20,21)

With respect to Eve, he writes:

"The whole creation has been groaning together in the pains of childbirth until now. And not only the creation, but we ourselves, who have the firstfruits of the Spirit, groan inwardly as we wait eagerly for adoption as sons, the redemption of our bodies."

(verses 22,23)

The frustration of Adam and the pain of Eve, shared by their sons and daughters, are ultimately redemptive. They reflect the frustration and pain of "the whole creation", and focus the mind first on the Son, then on "the sons of God": "The creation waits with eager longing for the revealing of the sons of God" (verse 19).

Desire and domination – a tragedy for their relationship

Frustration and pain were inflicted by God, for a purpose: "I will ..." But the next two lines reflect something not of God's doing. Sin would distort the lovely relationship that had existed between man and woman. Sadly He spoke of what would follow inevitably from their actions.

For her part, the woman would experience "desire". The unusual Hebrew word translated "desire", *teshuqah* occurs in post-biblical Hebrew with the meaning 'urge, craving, impulse'*; but it occurs only three times in Scripture. In the Song of Songs it is coupled with the Hebrew preposition *al*, and is used in a positive sense of the lover's attraction to his beloved: "his desire is for me" (7:10).

But in Genesis 4 it is coupled with the Hebrew preposition *el*, and is used in a negative sense when God admonishes Cain, "Sin is crouching at the door. Its desire is for you, but you must rule over it" (Genesis

---

*D Talley, in *The New Dictionary of Old Testament Theology and Exegesis*, vol 4, p 341.

4:7). Sin sought to take Cain as prey, to bring him under its dominion and impel him. Unless he mastered sin he would become its slave, a warning later echoed by David in words which draw on this incident:

> "Keep back your servant also from presumptuous sins; let them not have *dominion* over me! Then I shall be blameless, and innocent of great transgression." (Psalm 19:13)

Paul also warns similarly:

> "Let not sin therefore reign in your mortal bodies, to make you obey their passions ... Sin will have no dominion over you ... if you present yourselves to anyone as obedient slaves, you are slaves of the one whom you obey; either of sin, which leads to death, or of obedience which leads to righteousness ... What fruit were you getting at that time from the things of which you are now ashamed? The end of those things is death." (Romans 6:13-21)

Sin's impulse is to possess and control Cain; in response, God instructs him to master sin.

It is this same combination of noun and preposition that is used in Genesis 3, only a few verses earlier, and we believe that it should again be understood in a negative sense. Instead of being a complement and a help for man, Eve would wish to assert her own will, set her own independent agenda, possess and control the man.

The man, for his part, would "rule" (Hebrew, *mashal*) over his wife. Again, like "desire", "rule" is neither positive nor negative in itself. But it is telling that this is the same Hebrew word translated "dominion" in David's great psalm about God's purpose: "You have given him *dominion* over the works of your hands; you have put all things under his feet" (Psalm 8:6). This statement is based on God's words in the creation of man and woman, where the two of them were together given dominion over the whole creation as God's stewards.

Sin devastated this ideal. When Noah emerged from the ark, "dominion" over the creation as God's steward was replaced by "fear" and "dread" (Genesis 9:1,2). Sin was similarly devastating for the relationship between man and woman. Adam had been filled with recognition, appreciation, celebration, tender love and innocent pleasure when God had first brought Eve to him (2:22-25). Now God speaks of rulership. She is no longer an equal partner in dominion, but one of the creatures to be dominated – sinfully, the author hastens to add: for this was no part of God's purpose. The man would abandon the joyful, loving partnership that had been theirs, and would seek sinfully to rule over the woman, asserting himself, applying legal weight and physical force to dominate her for his own ends.

This interpretation has been adopted by some scholars and rejected by others, and we do not insist on it. But Paul's instruction that wives should respect and submit to their husbands, and that husbands should love and nurture their wives, appears to be his direct response to these new tensions foreseen by God.

Two objections

It is true that in the course of history women have rarely been able to assert themselves, and have generally been subservient to men. Only with the rise of radical second-wave feminism in the 1960s and 1970s have Western women truly broken free of male domination. Women in other cultures are yet to attain these levels of freedom. But this only underlines the reality of male domination, also a consequence of the sin-corrupted relationship.

It is also true that many women do not feel this way about their own relationships with men. No doubt many men would also say that they do not feel the desire to dominate their wives. The notorious 'battle of the sexes' suggests, however, that tension or open conflict between man and woman, husband and wife is a reality for many women and men, at least in human beings untouched by the regenerating grace of God. The rule of love in Paradise has been subverted by struggle and domination. These sinful emotions are not limited to the man–woman relationship. Sinful emotions like self-exaltation and pride can infect any relationship.

What is important, however, is to recognise that the cause of this conflict is sin; the explanation of it is the Fall; the answer to it lies in both husband and wife becoming new creatures in Christ, dedicated to loving and respecting one another. The fact that followers of Christ, taking Paul's advice to heart, do not feel these tensions in their relationship only highlights the importance and value of his instruction.

Terrible consequences

For most, however, the millennia since the Fall have been characterized by these profound consequences that cut across cultures in time and space. Male domination has led to enormous evils – endemic chauvinism, tyranny and repression in the family, the very frequent neglect of the needs and interests of children and women, the rampant sexualisation of society, and the dehumanization of women through pornography, sexual addiction, prostitution, relationship violence, sexual abuse, rape, female mutilation and female infanticide. The understandable reaction to these abuses has not been without its own consequences – the emasculation of men, the defeminisation of women, and the dehumanisation of the unborn child in abortion.

Truly, God has abandoned to themselves those who did not like to retain Him in their thoughts! Yet His very own are not free of these evils – though we ought to be. For neither the woman nor the man ought to behave in these ways. Usurpation and domination, the rebel and the tyrant, are no part of God's design. He had put in place a happy pairing of responsibility and valued help, but that had been corrupted. God did not intend these terrible consequences, but He did foresee them.

6

SCRIPTURAL ADVICE FOR
WIVES AND HUSBANDS

ADAM and Eve must have been the most perfectly matched couple in history, but Scripture is filled with marriages: for the union of one man and one woman for life, to the exclusion of all others was God's intention for human life until His Kingdom should come, when marriage will be no longer necessary. We know it will be replaced, for those who are counted worthy to obtain the resurrection and the kingdom will be like the angels, Jesus said, who neither marry nor are given in marriage. For now, however, marriage is normal to God's order.

God's first words to the man and the woman He had made were words of blessing: "Be fruitful and multiply and fill the earth" (Genesis 1:28). Sexual desire was therefore created "very good" in the beginning, and the consummation of marriage in "one flesh" (2:24) is a clear reference to sexual union. In its proper place it is still one of God's good things. The psychological and physical love-relationship between man and woman is celebrated in the Song of Songs, which has been interpreted in turn by many commentators as a fitting symbol of the loving relationship that should join Israel with her God, and the bride with Christ. There is no place in the Old or New Testaments for the asceticism that mistakenly sees something perverse in the sexual dimension of a loving husband–wife relationship. "Let marriage be held in honour among all, and let the marriage bed be undefiled" (Hebrews 13:4).

But there is no doubt that sexual desire has complicated the relationship between man and woman since the Fall: and it is one of the things that will fall away when we pass from corruption to incorruption.

26

When this tension is no longer present, extraordinarily deep friendships between men and women will be possible. Scripture says little about this. It is, as Robert Roberts once said, "a blessed secret". We can be certain that whatever is to come will be infinitely more satisfying than anything, any relationship, in this present life.

The most challenging of human relationships

Until that day, however, marriage is the most intimate, the most important and the most challenging human relationship that we experience. Most, that is: for some are naturally single, some are compelled to be single, and some choose to be single as an act of service, as Jesus observed (Matthew 19:12). Marriage is honourable. Singleness is also honourable; and we shall come to that next.

Scripture is filled with marriages, but not with many marriages that are entirely happy. We think immediately of Abraham and Sarah, whose outstanding relationship was not without its challenges, now brought on by Abraham's apprehension, now by Sarah's sensitivity or unbelief, now by their shared struggle to work out the will of God in promising a seed, now by their different ideas about how to deal with the inevitable tension between the bondwoman and her son, and the free woman and the child of promise. Their marriage was, ultimately, a great success, but it was far from easy. Isaac and Rebekah, an arranged marriage if ever there was one, were nevertheless strongly attracted to each other physically, and shared a deep commitment to the promises. Even then they were at odds as to who should inherit the blessing until Isaac with fear and trembling recognized the hand of God, and committed himself to Jacob.

It is fair to say that, while married couples feature in many of the Bible's stories, we do not have many marriages that are unmistakably happy and fruitful. Perhaps the union of Boaz and Ruth is the only instance we have in the Old Testament. In the New

Testament we have several more – Zacharias and Elizabeth, Joseph and Mary, Aquila and Priscilla – but there are not very many. Clearly, the most faithful men and women wrestle with the same issues that challenge all marriages.

The reasons are not hard to find. Sin has invaded every life, every garden. The image of God has been marred in man and woman, and the whole creation is affected. Self-will, greed, pride, even oppression, infidelity and violence are often found where mutual respect, selflessness, moderation, care, faithfulness, love and self-sacrifice ought to be. Marriage may be deeply satisfying for some, but it is wretched and miserable for others. We are not what we ought to be, and neither are our relationships.

New creatures, new relationships

But the renewing work of God reaches into every corner of life. The Lord Jesus knows nothing of a private world, a private life where he cannot go – unless, of course, we wish to bar the door against him, and ignore his persistent knocking. Paul urges us to "put off your old self, which belongs to your former manner of life and is corrupt through deceitful desires" (Ephesians 4:22), and, having a new mind, "to put on the new self".

The new man and the new woman are "after the likeness of God … created in true righteousness and holiness" (verse 24). Renewed creatures relate to each other in new ways. They put away lying, and they tell the truth, because they see themselves as integrally related, "members one of another" (verse 25). They regulate their anger (verses 26,27). Instead of stealing, they work and give (verse 28). Their words are purposefully upbuilding, ministering to others the grace they themselves have received (verse 29). Relationships are transformed: and marriage becomes something much greater.

Even where only one partner has come into Christ the effect can be dramatic. A brother is baptized, but his wife does not believe. A sister believes, but her husband does not. The marriage should stay together if at all possible, commanded the Lord: and Paul faithfully communicated that injunction (1 Corinthians 7:10,11). Paul, explaining Christ's command in more detail, provides further advice:

"The unbelieving husband is made holy because of his wife, and the unbelieving wife is made holy because of her husband. Otherwise your children would be unclean, but as it is, they are holy."

(verse 14)

Even where only one partner has been called by the Lord, the new relationship between the believer and the Lord fundamentally changes the spiritual status of the relationship with the unbelieving partner and their children. They now come under God's special care. In time they may enter Christ themselves, and be saved: who knows? (verse 16). The wife should not leave her husband, or vice versa, but should work with Christ to sanctify the continuing relationship.

To avoid any misunderstanding at this point, the author wishes to make it clear that he does not believe anything in the Word of God requires women to live with violence. Paul is not directly addressing that question in this place. His overarching message is that, in general, husbands and wives, circumcised and uncircumcised, slaves and free, married and unmarried should accept their position in life, and concentrate on what they can do in the service of Christ. "Let each person lead the life that the Lord has assigned to him, and to which God has called him" (verse 17; reiterated in verses 20,24).

"Heirs with you of the grace of life"

Peter gives similar advice. A wife should "be subject" to her own husband (1 Peter 3:1). It is the same word used of Jesus' submission to his parents (Luke 2:51), and is several times used of the attitude of a Christian wife to her husband (Ephesians 5:22,24; Colossians 3:18; Titus 2:5; 1 Peter 3:5). What is remarkable, however, is that Peter calls for this attitude even to husbands who "do

29

not obey the word". He uses the same language elsewhere in this letter of those who have refused the gospel (2:7,8; 3:20; 4:17). In other words, the wife should accept the husband's leadership in the family even when he is not a believer, and win him for Christ "without a word", preaching most eloquently by her exemplary conduct. Her chastity, respect, and restraint, her meek and quiet spirit will mark her out as a Christian woman. Not a word need be said. And "the hidden person of the heart", the undying image of Christ growing within from embryonic seed to mature perfection, would be highly prized by God, to whom she should look in faith.

Perhaps sisters need a model. So Peter directs their attention back to "the holy women", the faithful sisters of the Old Testament Scriptures, and picks out a prime example: "Sarah obeyed Abraham, calling him lord" (3:6). Peter's reference is to the time when three angels came to Abraham's encampment to announce that a child would be born to Sarah nine months from that day, "according to the time of life" (Genesis 18:14, KJV). Sarah, listening in the tent door, laughed in unbelief – not out loud, but "to herself". We know what she said, because the angels read her mind. "After I am worn out, and my lord is old, shall I have pleasure?" (verse 12). No words were said. Sarah was not even visible: she was in the tent doorway, out of the visitors' line of sight. There was nobody to impress. She was not even focused on Abraham. Her reference to him was incidental. Yet she called him "lord" in her heart: and that casual reference speaks volumes of her attitude to Abraham day by day. Sarah was a beautiful woman, despite her age: but her real beauty was her attitude, "the hidden person of the heart". That is how she adorned herself. Her thought, unbelieving as it was, nevertheless revealed an attitude of mind that was fundamentally oriented to God, and His will for her marriage. That is Peter's point. 'Do not fear: put your trust in God: submit yourself to your husband: do well: and you will be prized by God.'

Then Peter turns to husbands:

"Live with your wives in an understanding way, showing honour to the woman as the weaker vessel, since they are heirs with you of the grace of life, so that your prayers may not be hindered." (1 Peter 3:7) The understanding to which Peter refers is knowledge built on faith and virtue, the knowledge that leads to self-control, "the knowledge of our Lord and Saviour Jesus Christ" (2 Peter 1:5,6; 3:18). This knowledge should influence the way he lives with his wife, who is "the weaker vessel". In what sense Peter does not explicitly say, but the word means literally 'without strength' and often refers to physical weakness or even sickness (Matthew 25:39,43,44; Luke 10:9; Acts 4:9; 5:15,16; 1 Corinthians 11:30; 2 Corinthians 10:10). So the husband is not to use his greater strength to dominate his wife.

Although there is a general principle of respect and consideration here, Peter is speaking specifically of sexual relations. Similar language is used by Paul: "That each one of you know how to control his own body in holiness and honour; not in the passion of lust" (1 Thessalonians 4:4,5). Husbands and wives should be considerate of each other's sexual needs, and even spiritual activities such as "fasting and prayer" are no reason to deprive each other of mutual affection, intimacy and sexual satisfaction. Paul even refers to such deprivation as 'defrauding' or 'cheating', a term we would normally associate with infidelity (1 Corinthians 7:1-5). But the apostles are also conscious of a danger in the other direction: that the husband may be completely unreasonable in his demands, leaving the wife physically and psychologically exhausted. Paul, therefore, warns against unrestrained lustfulness; and Peter warns that husbands should show their wives, who are physically weaker, the greatest respect and consideration: especially, he says, seeing "they are heirs with you of the grace of life".

Peter is still thinking of Abraham and Sarah. The promises, "the grace of life", were to both of them, not as individuals, but as a married couple. It was impossible for them to inherit the promises in isolation from each other, for the promise would come through a child whom they would conceive together, and that child would be the fruit of faithful prayer. Only when Sarah had been challenged to share Abraham's resurrection faith – the faith that out of two dead bodies life would come – did the promise of God begin to work itself out in her body.

Our situation may not be theirs exactly: but the principles are most important. In Christ husband and wife have received the same gracious promises of God, and will inherit the same eternal life. God will hear their prayers if they put their trust in Him, and evidence that trust in the way they speak of each other, and treat each other. Peter is not threatening; but his implied warning underlines the seriousness with which God views our behaviour toward each other. If we do not treat each other with the greatest respect, He may shut His ears to our prayers.

"I speak concerning Christ and the ecclesia"

Paul's teaching echoes that of Peter:

"Wives, submit to your husbands, as is fitting in the Lord. Husbands, love your wives, and do not be harsh with them." (Colossians 3:18,19)

The young women are "to love their husbands and children, to be self-controlled, pure, working at home, kind, and submissive to their own husbands, that the word of God may not be reviled" (Titus 2:4,5).

But it is in his letter to the Ephesians that Paul expands on the relationship between husband and wife. After some detailed instruction about righteousness and holiness in interpersonal relationships generally, Paul turns to the most intimate relationship of all – marriage. Here, too, attitudes and behaviours typical of the old, sinful way of life must be replaced by those God always intended between husband and wife.

Mutual submission to each other in Christ is an attitude that comes with the new creature (Ephesians 5:21), and it should be evident also in marriage. There is no artificial divide between home, ecclesia and workplace. The new man or woman will show the same unified heart, mind, soul and strength wherever he or she goes.

And so the wife is instructed to submit herself to her husband "as to the Lord" (verse 22) "in everything" (verse 24). Later Paul uses a rather extreme term: "let the wife see that she respects (AV, "reverence") her husband" (verse 33). The Greek *phobos* means "fear". We do not imagine for one moment that Paul used the term in a literal sense. Nonetheless, it is an extreme term, and underlines the importance he attached to the respect a wife should show her husband.

But Paul gives much greater space to spelling out the husband's responsibility. He is the head of the wife, a position of authority (verse 23). How should he use it? As a strong-willed tyrant, making unreasonable demands, insisting on compliance, requiring unquestioning obedience, structuring every minute of family life around his own selfish preferences? Certainly not! As in Christ we are all free to serve, so the husband has authority to give himself in love to his wife:

> "Husbands, love your wives, as Christ loved the church and gave himself up for her, having cleansed her ... so that he might present the church to himself ... that she might be holy and without blemish."
>
> (verses 25-27)

Husbands are commanded to love, and the standard is no less than Christ's selfless – no, self-giving – love for his people. The focus is spiritual: to sanctify, to cleanse, to purify, to approve. Let every husband "examine himself, then, and so eat of the bread, and drink of the cup": for the Christ whom he comes to remember, before whom he presents himself, will note the spirit in which, through the week, that man has loved his bride.

"In the same way husbands should love their wives as their own bodies" (verses 28,29). Paul's argument has sometimes been misunderstood as an appeal to self-interest. Nothing could be further from the truth. Paul's appeal is to the example of Christ. How did Christ love his own body? He yielded it to the greatest agony and shame that he might breathe life into his bride. Now he has incorporated her into himself: "for we are members of his body, of his flesh, and of his bones" (verse 30, KJV). He "nourishes and cherishes" his body, that is, the ecclesia (verse 29), investing his mind, heart, soul and strength into preparing her for the day of accountability, perfection and glory.

Paul alludes to Genesis 2, and the first marriage. Yes, the relationship between Adam and Eve sets the pattern for all the marriages that should follow after: but it is itself based on a greater and prior pattern, "Christ and the church" (verses 31,32). Every marriage, therefore, should be inspired by the self-giving love and great respect that characterizes the relationship between the Son of God and his Bride. It is not to be paid lip-service as a general principle, but taken to heart as an individual charge:

"Let each one of you love his wife as himself; and let the wife see that she respects her husband."

(verse 33)

That Paul intended this as a direct response to the sinful corruption of the marriage relationship in Eden is also clear in the parallel passage:

"Wives, submit to your husbands, as is fitting in the Lord. Husbands, love your wives, and do not be harsh with them."   (Colossians 3:18,19)

It is of a piece with the Lord's conception of shepherd-leadership – that true authority works itself out in total service.

Paul's instruction is designed to meet the moral consequences of man's fall head on. Sin might have changed our circumstances dramatically, but God's intended roles for husband and wife have not changed.

By allowing God to recreate us, we can, through the blood of the Lamb, rebuild the first, loving relationship between Adam and Eve, and drive sin from love's garden.

What husband looks to the day of Christ, and works single-mindedly to nurture and cherish his wife, not only in this life, but for that which is to come? That man truly understands what Christ has done for him.

Another gift, of singleness

At other times Paul argues in favour of singleness. For most disciples, this is impassable, not to mention perilous, terrain. But for those who can receive it, singleness can "secure undistracted devotion to the Lord" (1 Corinthians 7:35, NASB). It is "even better" than marriage in the Lord (verses 37,38), and the God-ordained status of immortals in His Kingdom. Those who remain single, by choice or circumstance (Matthew 19:12), can serve the Lord positively, freely, flexibly, effectively. Singleness comes with self-denial and loneliness, but it can also lead to an extraordinary focus on God. It has many Scriptural examples in Joshua, Elijah and Elisha, Anna, John the Baptist, Paul – and, of course, the perfect example in every sense, our Lord Jesus Christ.

He was a single man, and he was also the most complete manifestation of our Heavenly Father. He came to minister – to the lonely, the sick and infirm, the outcast, the needy, the aged and the youthful. His relationships crossed natural and social barriers – Peter, James and John; Zacchaeus; Mary and Martha; Nicodemus and Joseph of Arimathaea. He dedicated himself utterly in service to his Father, and he touched lives emotionally and spiritually. He remained unmarried and sinless, and he is our example and inspiration.

The relationship between Christ and the ecclesia is mirrored in the marriage relationship, but we are not men and women, or brethren and sisters, by virtue of marriage. We express ourselves as men and women, and connect as brothers and sisters, whether we are married or unmarried. Men and women are intended to complement each other, whether they are bound by marriage or not. It is possible in singleness, as in marriage, to work out the purpose of God for man and woman in the ecclesia and, in different ways, in the home.

7

AS THE LAW ALSO SAYS

WE might be anxious to press on to the time of the Lord Jesus and the apostles, to begin our examination of their teaching. But we cannot simply hurdle the two-thirds of the Bible written in Hebrew, as if it were somehow not quite the word of God.

If it were so, why is Matthew at pains, on the first page of his gospel, to trace the origins of the Lord Jesus back through the years to Abraham and Sarah, and to demonstrate that the coming of the Lord Jesus fulfilled a prophecy made 700 years before about a virgin who was to conceive a child who would be the living presence of God among us, and rescue his people from the consequences of their sins?

And if it were so, why do we find John, on the last page of what is revealed by God to His servants, referring to "your brothers the prophets"? Why is the Lord Jesus "the root and the descendant of David"? And why is he holding out the prospect of eating from the tree of life?

"The New is in the Old instilled:
The Old is in the New fulfilled."

Walking the road to Emmaus with two friends, the Lord Jesus, "beginning with Moses and all the Prophets … interpreted to them in all the Scriptures the things concerning himself" (Luke 24:27). The effect was extraordinary. Their hearts were fired with powerful new insights into what we call "the Old Testament". Suddenly they were seeing what had been stamped on those pages from the beginning – the image of the Son of God.

Later that night he revealed himself in the midst of the astonished disciples:

> "Then he said to them, 'These are my words that I spoke to you while I was still with you, that everything written about me in the Law of Moses and the Prophets and the Psalms must be fulfilled.' Then he opened their minds to understand the Scriptures, and said to them, 'Thus it is written ...'"
>
> (Luke 24:44,45)

If this were the practice of the Lord Jesus, then should not we, his brothers and sisters, seek understanding on every page of the God-breathed Word – "in the Law of Moses and the Prophets and the Psalms"?

Yet it is not always easy for us to understand the genius of those parts of the Bible written originally in Hebrew "by inspiration of God". The psalms we can readily relate to; and the wisdom literature; and the prophets; and the narratives, patterned with obedience and disobedience, reformation and decay. But the Lord Jesus began at Moses, as we have done: and we shall continue with Moses a little longer, moving from Genesis to the Law.

"Why then the law?"

> "A person is not justified by works of the law but through faith in Jesus Christ ... we also have believed in Christ Jesus, in order to be justified by faith in Christ and not by works of the law, because by works of the law no one will be justified."
>
> (Galatians 2:16)

> "For through the law I died to the law, so that I might live to God."   (verse 19)

> "If justification were through the law, then Christ died for no purpose."   (verse 21)

> "All who rely on works of the are under a curse."
>
> (3:10)

> "No one is justified before God by the law."
>
> (verse 11)

> "The law is not of faith."   (verse 12)

"Christ redeemed us from the curse of the law."
(verse 13)

"If the inheritance comes by the law, it no longer comes by promise." (verse 18)

It is not surprising that after such a shattering broadside Paul should sense some bewilderment in the minds of his readers; and on their behalf he asks one of his characteristic rhetorical questions, "Why then the law?" (verse 19). What, indeed, was the purpose of this comprehensive system of priesthood, worship and sacrifice, moral justice and civil regulation? Why had God allowed it to stand for so long? Why had He delivered it into Israel's hands in the first place?

The answer, says Paul, is that the Law played an important supporting role in the drama of salvation. "It was added because of transgressions, until the offspring should come to whom the promises were made." It did not cut across the promises. It did not give life, because life is God's gift: it cannot be purchased by our good works. But "before faith came" the Law acted as prison warden, guardian, tutor and governor. It restrained sin. It shepherded the people of God on their way to faith. It taught them – taught them in elaborate detail – about the "better thing" that was to come. It regulated their daily life until they were ready for the freedom and responsibility that come with spiritual maturity.

We must remember these purposes when we look at the Law, or we shall lose our balance. In his writings Paul is generally negative in his statements about the Law, and rightly so, because he is desperately keen to ensure that his readers do not turn their back on faith and grace, and retreat into that which had become familiar and comfortable after 1,600 years. And he is equally keen, no doubt, to ensure that later readers do not pervert the gospel they have received – salvation by a living, trustful faith in God and His righteousness into self-salvation by formal membership and outward show.

But it is also Paul who says in a letter which is arguably the comprehensive development of Galatians, the "commandment … promised life" (Romans 7:10). "The law is holy, and the commandment is holy and righteous and good" (verse 12). "The law is spiritual" (verse 14). "I agree with the law, that it is good" (verse 16). "I delight in the law of God, in my inner being" (verse 22). "I myself serve the law of God with my mind" (verse 25). "He condemned sin in the flesh, in order that the righteous requirement of the law might be fulfilled in us, who walk not according to the flesh but according to the Spirit" (8:3,4). "The mind that is set on the flesh is hostile to God, for it does not submit to God's law; indeed, it cannot" (verse 7).

"I am not come to destroy, but to fulfil"

Despite its limited purpose, therefore, God revealed Himself and His Son in the Law. For one-and-a-half thousand years, that is how God's people came to know and love Him. In fact, as the Lord Jesus himself makes clear, love is the foundation of the Law. Love, far from being alien to the Law, is best expressed in the terms of the Law itself, "You shall love the Lord your God", and "You shall love your neighbour as yourself" (Matthew 7:12; 19:17-19; 22:37-40). The Lord's teaching is endorsed by James (2:8) and Paul (Galatians 5:14; Romans 13:9,10; 1 Timothy 1:5).

Similarly with the New Covenant. It is a spiritual creature not of the New Testament, but of the Old. It is new not in the apostles, but in the prophets; and far from rendering the Law irrelevant, the first term of the New Covenant, as Jeremiah tells us, is that God will write His law indelibly upon the hearts of "the house of Israel", by this means binding them to Him as His people and fulfilling His promise to Abraham, "I will be their God" (Jeremiah 31:33,34, cp. Genesis 17:1-8).

It is evident that many in the crowd about Jesus misunderstood his attitude to the Law. So in a few plain words, he cleared it up. "Do not think that I have come to destroy the Law or the Prophets; I have not come to

40

abolish them but to fulfil them" (Matthew 5:17). Christ has not consigned the law, or the prophets, to the dustbin. Rather, they have been perfectly expressed in him: and in him they have enduring relevance to those who seek to know him, and the righteousness which is of God by faith. The Master underlines his point by adding that those who teach otherwise are chancing their salvation. It is no light matter.

We have written at some length and with some force on this theme because there is a tendency in some quarters to minimise the Old Testament, to treat it as if it were little more than a prologue to the New, and no longer relevant to Christians in the twenty-first century. That is very far from the truth. We are not to divide the God of the Bible, as did the Gnostic cults of the second century, into a deity of the Old Testament, legalistic, harsh, wrathful, even barbaric, and a deity of the New, gentle and easy to be intreated. "The LORD our God, the LORD is one" (Deuteronomy 6:4). "There is … one God and Father of all" (Ephesians 4:6).

The living Word of God is likewise one integral whole, and that whole is "profitable for teaching, for reproof, for correction, and for training in righteousness, that the man of God may be competent, equipped for every good work" (2 Timothy 3:16,17). While the New Testament was taking shape as Paul wrote, it is the Old Testament from which Timothy had learned his faith, and the Old Testament that is front of mind for Paul in this important statement of the inspiration of Scripture – "all Scripture".

Rightly understood, therefore, the Old Testament still has relevant and important things to teach us about the relationship between man and woman in the purpose of God. And that is why, despite the plain teaching of the word of God that we are in no sense under the Law, or bound by it, it has great value for us today, and "every scribe who has been trained for the kingdom of heaven" will find treasure in it, as in other parts of the Bible.

8

WOMEN UNDER THE LAW

WHAT, then, are we to make of those provisions of the Law which relate specifically to women? There are passages where women are apparently spoken of as property. For example, they are listed among a man's assets, not to be coveted by his neighbour (Exodus 20:17). A man might sell his daughters into slavery (21:7-11). A man who seduced a virgin was required to compensate her father (22:16; Deuteronomy 22:28,29). These passages are not confined to women. Male servants are also spoken of as in some sense property. We find these passages challenging not because of the treatment of women only, but the treatment of any human being as some form of property.

Then there are provisions where women are punished for immoral conduct. A woman could be stoned if found not to be a virgin at marriage (Deuteronomy 22:13-21), or if caught in adultery (verse 22), or if caught sleeping with a man other than her betrothed before marriage (verses 23,24). A suspicious husband could compel his wife to undergo the jealousy ritual (Numbers 5:11-31). Again, while these provisions are specific to women, all manner of sins were dealt with sternly under the Law, and both man and woman were equally liable to capital punishment in the case of adultery (Leviticus 20:10-21).*

---

* We know of only one occasion where an adulterer was confronted with his sin, and that was David. While God's holiness must be understood and endorsed, it is wonderfully comforting to note His immediate forgiveness of this guilty man as soon as he confessed his sin. In other respects – examples include the treatment of property crime, the natural environment, debt and poverty – the Law is arguably ahead of today's jurisprudence.

"For the hardness of your hearts"

Then there are provisions where the mistreatment of women is apparently accepted and tolerated. For example, a man dissatisfied with his wife due to "some uncleanness" could divorce her (Deuteronomy 24:1-4). A woman taken captive in war could be taken in marriage (21:10-14). Wives could be multiplied, although the rights of the first wife were specially protected (21:15-17), as were the rights of concubines (Exodus 21:7-11).

It should be noted that virtually none of the practices listed above were instituted by the Law. They were strongly entrenched in Middle Eastern society well before the Law. And here the Lord Jesus gives us an important insight into the mind of God. When questioned by the religious leaders of his day – some of whom considered it entirely justifiable to divorce a woman for such trivial 'offences' as speaking too loudly, or burning the bread – the Lord Jesus replied:

> "Because of your hardness of your heart he [Moses] wrote you this commandment. But from the beginning of creation, God made them male and female … What therefore God has joined together, let not man separate." (Mark 10:2-9)

The regulation of divorce

God's will was undoubtedly the harmonious companionship of man and woman in Eden. The reality was that far too many Israelite men had hard hearts, and the women in their lives suffered the consequences. The situation was not about to change quickly, for the coming of Jesus Christ was a long way off. In the meantime, therefore, God would do what He could, within the limitations of their society, to alleviate the worst suffering of women who had been rejected by their husbands.

The arrangements for divorce are typical. God did not institute divorce. In truth, He hated it (Malachi 2:13-16). It was a human invention, one more sad demonstration of the truth of what God had forecast –

that men would sinfully dominate women. But God did regulate divorce in three important ways.

First, He limited the grounds for divorce, preventing women from being cut loose at the whim of their husbands. He completely prohibited divorce in the case of a woman raped or seduced before marriage (Deuteronomy 22:28). Second, God insisted on provision of a "certificate of divorce". The formal documentation would confirm the woman's legal freedom and make remarriage legally possible. In the same way a prisoner of war could not be sold into slavery if her husband tired of her: she must be set free (21:14). Third, He strictly prohibited the husband from taking the divorced woman back if he changed his mind, a provision honoured even in the morally loose days of Jeremiah (Jeremiah 3:1). This prohibition would discourage casual divorce by a mercurial husband, and reduce the danger of women being treated as playthings by the rich and powerful.

It is not in divorce, but in the regulation of divorce, that God's character traits of faithfulness and mercy are evident. Marriage was intended to be for life. Relationships were to be committed, not capricious. Difficulties were to be worked through together. Women, though relatively powerless in that society, were not to be thrown into the street at the whim of their husbands. They were to be treated with respect, and cared for. Hard hearts must at least be restrained, if they could not be softened.

Stepping-stones to grace and faith

These provisions are among many in the Law which were designed to protect those with relatively little power in Israelite society – women, orphans, the poor, and "strangers" from other nations living among them. In these provisions those of faith would see God's character and will, and live well above the minimum standards set, feeling their way toward the full revelation of God in Jesus Christ.

Finally, there are those passages in which the will of women is constrained or subordinated to the will of their fathers or husbands in some way. A woman's vow could be disallowed by her father or her husband (Numbers 30:3-8). The daughters of Zelophehad were granted inheritance rights, but must marry only within the tribe of Manasseh (Numbers 36). A widow without children was to be married to her husband's relative to perpetuate her husband's family name (Deuteronomy 25:5-10). These provisions also reflect cultural realities: but again, God's character is seen in the way established attitudes and practices were qualified and controlled by the Law.

Until Israel should be ready for spiritual freedom and responsibility, the provisions of the Law would serve God's purposes – restraining sin, shepherding the people of God on their way to faith, teaching them about the 'better thing' to come, and regulating their daily life. Within that framework God revealed His righteousness and love, easing the lot of women where it was possible to do so: but sin would continue to reign until faith and grace should come, and with them a new creation.

9

PARABLES IN ACTION

THERE are other aspects of the Law, however, which cannot be understood in this way. Take, for example, the provisions surrounding childbirth.

Ritually unclean

The mother was ritually unclean for a period after the birth. She was prohibited from attending the sanctuary in that time, and was also required to offer sacrifice at the end of the period (Leviticus 12:6-8). It is possible that God intended this, at least in part, to protect the health of the new mother – but the regulations go further. When a woman had given birth to a son, she was ritually unclean for 40 days. When she had given birth to a daughter, she was ritually unclean for 80 days (verses 2-5). What could be the meaning of the difference?

Reproduction taboos were probably entrenched in Middle Eastern society before the Law (cp. Genesis 31:35), and menstruation, sex and other discharges of body fluids were also classified as ritually unclean. This ritual uncleanness was probably intended to draw attention to an important moral truth – that the human life which had been perpetuated through conception and birth was tainted by sin at the point where life began.

This understanding may lie behind David's heartfelt confession, "I was brought forth in iniquity; and in sin did my mother conceive me" (Psalm 51:5). Presumably David was born in wedlock, and neither of his statements were literally true: both, however, authentically express the profound sense of sinfulness and guilt that David experienced as a result of his sexually motivated crimes against Uriah, Bathsheba – and ultimately, God. His statement foreshadows that of the Lord Jesus, "Why do you call me good? No one is good but one, that is, God" (Matthew 19:17, NKJV) – and this from the truly extraordinary Son of God, who always outworked his Father's will to perfection, but nevertheless knew the true power of temptation from within and without.

We are not told explicitly why the birth of a daughter was followed by a double period of uncleanness. If the suggested interpretation of this symbolism is correct, perhaps we are intended to reflect on the fact that the baby girl would (in most circumstances) become a mother herself in time, giving birth in her turn to yet more sinners: and so the weary cycle of sin and death would continue, fulfilling the words of Genesis 3.

This and other similar provisions should not, therefore, be interpreted as a gratuitous slight on women, but understood rather as a ritual expression of an important moral truth, one way of highlighting the entrenched problem of sin and death in a framework that pointed forward to the coming of salvation, righteousness and life in the Son of God, "born of woman, born under the law", but a new thing nevertheless, compassed by the Spirit of God, and empowered to shatter that which held us in bondage.

The Nazirite vow

The Nazirite vow was created by God as an opportunity for Israelites who were not priests to enter upon a period of personal dedication. Its setting in the early chapters of Numbers suggests that God saw it as a crowning commitment to holiness. God's grace and peace were bestowed by His high priest and experienced by His people only after the details of the vow have been spelled out.

The most distinctive feature of Nazirites was their long hair, an echo of the high priest's *nezer,* or 'crown', on which was inscribed the words, "Holiness to the LORD". But the Nazirite continued to be subject to God's high priest, a fact underlined by the priest's leading role in the sacrifices offered on completion of the vow. But the details of the vow emphasise a parallel truth, that the sincere personal dedication of the Nazirite transcended the priesthood, which was inherited by right of birth and adherence to ritual and was not the outcome of a personal commitment to holiness on the part of the priest. The priesthood was "a legal requirement concerning bodily descent" (Hebrews 7:16); the Nazirite vow was a voluntary spiritual commitment.

Thus the priest abstained from wine only while on active duty in the Tabernacle; wore the turban and its golden plate only in the Holy Place, and avoided contact with death only while anointed with special oil. By contrast, the Nazirite avoided all contact with the vine and its fruits, wore the living crown of hair, avoided all contact with death – at all times while the vow was in force.

God's purpose with Israel was that they should be "a kingdom of priests and a holy nation" (Exodus 19:6). Israel was never prepared to make that kind of national commitment, and the inauguration of Aaron and his sons as priests was a recognition of that reality. Yet individual Israelites were not excluded. There were many ways in which they could live close to God, and His holiness; and if they were prepared to make a special voluntary commitment, then the Nazirite vow was graciously provided as a means.

And it was open to all Israelites:

> "When either a man or a woman makes a special vow, the vow of a Nazirite, to separate himself to the LORD ..." (Numbers 6:1,2)

A man or a woman could take on the vow; a man or a woman could accept the implications of the vow for daily life. No difference was made. A man or a woman, completing the vow, would shave their head, offer their sacrifices, and resume normal life.

Among the regulations of the Law the Nazirite vow is a striking statement of the voluntary spiritual dedication that God sought in all his children, male and female alike. It points both forward and back: back to the time when God created man male and female in His image and likeness, and forward to the time when in Christ we should all be members of "a chosen race, a royal priesthood, a holy nation, a people for his own possession" (1 Peter 2:9,10). It is one aspect of the Law's own testimony to the time when it should disappear before the rising glory of the Son of God, and the better things we have in him.

10

"THE HOLY WOMEN WHO HOPED IN GOD"

THE narratives of God's works and ways also have much to tell us about relationships between man and woman after the Fall, among the people of God.

Priests, prophets and kings

On the human side this inspired history is dominated by the men, faithful and faithless, who served as priests and Levites, judges and prophets, elders and kings, servants and masters, warriors and statesmen. God's intention that the man should lead at home and in the community is seen throughout this history.

But there are also "the holy women who hoped in God"; and it will be helpful to pause and consider them.

Sarah – the heart laid bare

Sarah first: for if Abraham is the father of all those who seek God and His righteousness by faith (Romans 4:11), then surely Sarah is their mother (Isaiah 51:1,2). She turned her back on civilization and joined Abraham in his epic journey, for love's sake believing all things, hoping all things, enduring all things.

But their relationship was not trouble-free. There was, for example, the first time they journeyed into Egypt. Sarah was exceptionally beautiful, and at some point it had crossed Abraham's mind that somebody might be moved to kill him, and take his wife for themselves. He had therefore instructed Sarah that she was to present herself as his sister (Genesis 12:11-13; 20:11-13). This was true, in a sense: Terah was her father, as he was Abraham's father. But they had different mothers: and the statement covered up the much more important truth that she was Abraham's wife. Abraham was indeed the father of the faithful, by God's own estimation: but he had moments of insecurity, and in one such moment he devised this intentional deception, this lie.

We might wonder how Sarah felt. Her husband, whom she clearly loved and respected, was prepared to deny his relationship with her to save his skin. We may suppose that she felt humiliated and anxious, but she followed the script. It worked all too well. Pharaoh took her into his harem. Eventually the truth emerged. Pharaoh was understandably resentful and angry. He rebuked Abraham, and ordered his men to see the Hebrews over the border. Abraham returned to "Bethel to the place where his tent had been at the beginning ... to the place where he had made an altar at the first." After faith's lapse in Egypt, Abraham returned to his spiritual roots, recovering and renewing his faith at the house of God (see Genesis 12:10–13:4).

Twenty-five years later the pattern repeated itself, this time in Gerar, a principality on the edge of the desert. Again Sarah cooperated. Abimelech took her into his harem. Again the truth emerged, this time through a direct revelation to the king in a dream. Abimelech's reaction differed from Pharaoh's. He was aghast at the near-disaster, but wanted an ongoing relationship with Abraham. He showered him with gifts, but rebuked Sarah for willingly cooperating in the deception. "Thus she was reproved" (Genesis 20).

There were other times of tension, such as the experiment with Hagar, instigated by Sarah, resulting in the conception and birth of Ishmael (Genesis 16:2,6); and Sarah's demand, fifteen or so years afterward, that the servant woman and her son be expelled from the camp (Genesis 21:10-12). Sarah was a strong woman, and she was well able to express her wishes when she wanted action. But in each case the final decision clearly lay with Abraham.

51

The apostle Peter, however, focuses on one incident that is indicative of their day-to-day relationship, and highlights Sarah's attitude as a model for women of faith.

It was the time when the angels visited Abraham and announced that a child would be born to Sarah twelve months later. Abraham believed: Sarah, listening from the darkness of the tent, gave vent to a cynicism engendered by decades of frustration, and silently jeered the declaration. God's messenger challenged her lack of faith, and reaffirmed the promise.

But Peter draws attention to Sarah's unspoken thoughts: "After I am worn out, and my lord is old, shall I have pleasure?" (Genesis 18:12). Never mind her lapse of faith, says Peter: note the fact that in her heart she called her husband "lord". She did not know that anybody had overheard her statement. In fact, she was rather panicked when she found the angels had heard her thoughts, and she attempted to deny them!

While the incident reveals her as decidedly human, despite the great faithfulness that characterised her life, it also emphasises her complete sincerity in thinking of and speaking of Abraham as her "lord". This "hidden person of the heart" was her true adornment, Peter insists, an investment in that meek, quiet and trustful spirit which is highly valued by God, and incorruptible: and he commends her example to all her spiritual daughters.

He has a word for husbands as well: and is it reasonable to see in this a reference to Abraham? He is certainly revealed in the context of this incident as a man whose prayers were fervent and effectual, who dwelt with his wife "in an understanding way", instructing "his children and his household after him to keep the way of the LORD by doing righteousness and justice, so that the LORD may bring to Abraham what he has promised him." – the promises which were for him "the grace of life".

Miriam – a powerful lesson in submission

Miriam is another signal woman of faith, whose courage and initiative, in faithfully watching over Moses and summoning her mother to care for the child, we remember from our earliest years.

Miriam was a natural leader. She was, with Moses and Aaron, an integral member of the team whom God "sent before" His people (Micah 6:4), and she made an important contribution to the momentous work of redeeming His people out of "the house of slavery", creating them a nation at Sinai, and bringing them safely through the desert to the borders of the Promised Land. She is identified as a prophetess, and led "all the women" in praise and dance, celebrating God's great act of deliverance and victory at the Red Sea (Exodus 15:20,21).

Tragically, an envious rivalry crept into her relationship with Moses. A mere three days (Numbers 10:33) after the host set out from Mount Sinai, a deadly contagion broke out in the camp – a plague of murmuring. It began among the people, presumably "in some outlying parts of the camp", where God's rebuke was first felt (11:1-3). "The rabble" began to long for what they had left behind in Egypt, and "the children of Israel" quickly took up the theme (11:4-10). Moses gave way to resentment and disbelief (11:10-15), and even Joshua was infected with competitive jealousy (11:28-30). A great abundance of quails only brought out the worst in the people, who were so frenzied that they accumulated an extraordinary excess – the minimum gathered by one was enough for ten – and tore into them without the least thought of thanks to the God who had provided (11:31-35).

And Miriam and Aaron, too, gave way to this evil spirit of discontent (Numbers 12:1). "Miriam and Aaron spoke against Moses." The references to Moses in the third person indicate that their unjustified complaints were expressed in the camp, as they lobbied other leaders, and manoeuvred for position. Miriam is mentioned first. She is also the one on whom God's hand fell heavily. Clearly she took the lead. The sister and brother attacked Moses' marriage to undermine his credibility and authority: a despicable tactic at any time. But Zipporah was a secondary target. Their real motive was embedded in their complaint:

> "Has the LORD indeed spoken only through Moses? Has he not spoken through us also?" (verse 2)

Miriam was a prophetess: Aaron was a prophet, and God's spokesman to Pharaoh. The words were objectively true. But there is no mistaking their intent: it was a bid for equality with their younger brother. They wanted more influence, more authority, more recognition.

The notice of Moses' meekness (verse 3) implies that he did not respond to their attack. Perhaps their politicking won them a hearing among the less discerning elders. But they had entirely forgotten their king, God Himself: "the LORD will reign forever and ever" (Exodus 15:18). They had not stopped to think that Moses had been chosen by God for service. It had never occurred to them that God was listening as they pressed their case. Unexpectedly, He interrupted them: "Suddenly the LORD said ... Come out, you three, to the tent of meeting" (Numbers 12:4).

God's rebuke was devastating. Yes, there were prophets – and Miriam and Aaron were not alone in that, as seventy new prophets had been created only recently (chapter 11). "If there is a prophet" – and the conditional clause underlines God's absolute prerogative – "I the LORD make myself known to him in a vision; I speak with him in a dream" (12:6). Moses was entirely different. As God's outstandingly faithful servant, charged with giving "food at the proper time" to the household, he had a unique relationship with God. "With him I speak mouth to mouth, clearly, and not in riddles, and he beholds the form of the LORD" (verses 7,8). How could they have been so bold as to challenge God's choice, and speak against him?

"The anger of the LORD was kindled against them" (verse 9). Perhaps God was incensed by their challenge. Perhaps, as in the case of Uzziah, judgment was triggered not by the initial fault, but by a proud refusal to accept that they had been wrong. Whatever the case, as the visible presence of God moved away, Aaron was shocked and horrified to see his sister riddled with leprosy. He learned wisdom in a moment, unreservedly confessed their sin, and appealed to Moses to intercede with God for her cure; which he promptly did. God relented, but as a mark of Miriam's disgrace, she was shut out of the camp for seven days; and progress toward the Promised Land halted altogether while God made His point.

We assume that Miriam returned to the camp in a different frame of mind and contributed helpfully throughout her life, but the facts are that nothing more is heard of her until her death (Numbers 20:1). She is named only once in Deuteronomy, as a cautionary tale: "Remember what the LORD your God did to Miriam" (24:9). Thankfully, she is mentioned positively again in Micah, and we are able to remember her for what she undoubtedly was: a faithful sister and a prophetess, who gave way to envy in a moment of discontent, and taught us all a signal lesson about accepting God's will for His people.

Deborah – wisdom as a woman

Deborah was another notable woman of faith, who judged Israel during a period of twenty years' oppression by Jabin of Hazor. "She used to sit under the palm tree of Deborah between Ramah and Bethel in the hill country of Ephraim, and the children of Israel came up to her for judgment' (Judges 4:4,5). In an inspired song celebrating God's victory over Jabin and his general Sisera, she called herself "a mother in Israel" (5:7). Her reference to "you who ride on white donkeys, you who sit on rich carpets" (5:10) is probably a reference to those who should have provided leadership (10:4; 12:14): but where were they when Israel desperately needed them? There was a leadership gap, and Deborah, prophetess and judge,* was called by God to provide godly civic guidance during that anarchic age when every man, every community, every tribe did "that which was right in its own eyes", without a thought for God's honour or the national good.

The time for action came. By inspiration Deborah called on Barak the son of Abinoam to lead a militia against Jabin's war host. He was willing to go, but only if she went with him. This she consented to do, but in a rebuke to his reluctant faith, and to the men of Israel more generally, she forewarned him that God would so arrange things that a woman would have the honour of inflicting final defeat on the brutal and sensual Sisera (4:8,9).

The critical importance of Deborah's work in an otherwise leaderless time cannot be overstated. She was one in a tradition of 'wise women', whose wisdom and counsel were highly valued in Israel (cf also 2 Samuel 14:2; 20:16), and who are celebrated in the wise and virtuous women of Proverbs (1:20-33; 3:13-18; 4:1-9; 8:1–9:12; 31:1-31). The comments of Robert Roberts, cited earlier, are worth recalling:

> "You can no more suppress a wise woman's influence and a wise woman's voice than you can suppress the law of gravitation ... you cannot prevent her giving good counsel, and you ought not ... I have seen tyrannical and unsympathetic men wrongly using Paul's authority to put down and quench godly women more qualified than they themselves to exercise judgment and give counsel ... We ought to be thankful when women turn up who are able to help with wise suggestion.' **

---

* Note that the NIV inaccurately renders the Hebrew *shaphat* in this place: "Deborah ... was leading Israel at that time." The verse should be translated, "Deborah was judging", as in the NIV margin, and the KJV, NKJV, RSV, NASB and ESV .

** "A voyage to Australia, New Zealand, and other lands", *The Christadelphian* 34(2) (February 1897): 60.

But it is also important to note the record's incidental references to the way Deborah operated. She did not set out on a regular circuit of judging and teaching as Samuel later did (1 Samuel 7:15-17). She was available and accessible "under the palm tree of Deborah", and Israelites came to her for her opinions and decisions (Judges 4:5). When the time came for action, she did not take the lead like an Ehud or a Jephthah, a Gideon or a Samson. Instead, she communicated the prophetic word of God to Barak, and agreed, at his request, to be present and provide moral support in fulfilling what was clearly his commission to lead Israel (4:6-9). As the story is later told by Samuel (1 Samuel 12:11) and in Hebrews (11:23), Barak is remembered for accepting her call to action.

We have focused on just three outstanding women of the Old Testament: Sarah, whose godly submission God overheard, making her, in a moment of doubt, a benchmark for godly women of all time; Miriam, honoured when she supported Moses, shamed when she challenged him for the leadership; Deborah, prophetess and judge, whose wisdom was seen not only in her celebrated counsel, but in the way she gave it.

There are many more: but these women illustrate important aspects of God's purpose in creating man male and female, and underline the critical contribution that women of faith made to the spiritual life of the people of God over the millennia between the call of Abraham and the coming of the Lord Jesus – and may still make.

11

JUDAISM AND WOMEN

WE shall look at Jesus' own attitude to women shortly: but to provide some context, we shall first look at the way his contemporaries varied the Law's treatment of women, as they did so many other provisions, with the effect of further enhancing the status of men and extending their control over women.

Reduced access to spiritual activity

In the Tabernacle of Moses and the Temple of Solomon women had been able to worship God in the same way as men. In the Temple of Herod, however, they were confined to the Court of the Women (Josephus, *Antiquities of the Jews* 15.418,419). Under the Law, husbands could disallow the vows of a wife or a daughter upon first hearing of them, but not otherwise. By the time of Jesus husbands could annul any vow, and could in fact force vows upon their wives (Mishnah, *Ketuboth* 7.1ff). In his day it had also become unusual or even forbidden for women to lay their hands on the head of sacrificial animals, or wave portions of the sacrifice before God (Tosephta, *Menahoth* 10.13,17, 528), even though this participation was expressly provided for in the Law.

Women were also excluded from daily spiritual activity. Schools were limited to boys. Women could participate in the synagogue service, but the scribal exposition of the Law which followed was restricted to males. Women were excused from daily prayer, and were not counted among the number of persons present at the recitation of blessings after a meal. Women were also excused from the annual festivals, although they could attend if they wished.

Societal discrimination

In an echo of the twist put upon the practice of *korban*, the law permitting divorce on grounds of 'some indecency' (Hebrew *erwat dabar*, Deuteronomy 24:1) was interpreted by Rabbi Hillel to refer first to 'unchastity' (*erwat*) and second to 'anything' (*dabar*), a view which had prevailed by the days of Jesus. Josephus championed this teaching, and in fact divorced his own wife because he was "not pleased with her behaviour" (*Life,* 426).

Men took priority over women in other ways. There was no essential difference between "the acquisition of a wife and the acquisition of a slave" (Jerusalem Talmud, *Ketuboth* 5.4). A man must generally be rescued before a woman, and the restoration of his lost property must come first (Mishnah, *Horayoth* 3.7). Josephus quotes as Scripture, "A woman is inferior to her husband in all things" (*Against Apion* 2.201), a statement nowhere to be found in the Old Testament.

Women were largely confined to home. Household duties were prescribed as a safeguard against adultery, and women ventured out only in outfits similar to those worn today by the most observant Muslim women, although the rules were of necessity relaxed for working-class families and in rural areas.*

Seen as naturally inclined to immorality

Judaism also began to see women as naturally inclined to immorality. While the Bible warns about the danger of adultery, it does not transfer the blame for sexual immorality from men to women. Furthermore, wisdom is personified as a woman throughout Proverbs, and the woman of wisdom is celebrated in the last chapter.

---

* These references, and many more, are summarized in J Jeremias (1969), '*Appendix: The social position of women*', chapter 18, *Jerusalem in the Time of Jesus* (London, SCM): 359-376. Quotations have been independently verified as far as possible.

But Judaism thought otherwise:

"Better is the churlishness of a man than a courteous woman, a woman, I say, which bringeth shame and reproach." (Ecclesiasticus 42:14)

"Of the woman came the beginning of sin, and through her we all die." (25:24)

"Rabbi Eliezer says: If a man gives his daughter a knowledge of the Law it is as though he taught her lechery. Rabbi Joshua says: A woman has more pleasure in one measure with lechery than in nine measures with modesty." (Mishnah, *Sotah* 3.4)

"Better to burn the Torah than to teach it to women." (Jerusalem Talmud, *Sotah* 3.4)

"Woe to him whose children are daughters." (Babylonian Talmud, *Kiddushin* 82b)

"And the Lord blessed Abraham in all things: What is the meaning of 'in all things'? Rabbi Meir says, 'He had no daughter.'" (Babylonian Talmud, *Kiddushin* 5.17)

"There are three benedictions which one must say every day: 'Blessed be He who did not make me a Gentile'; 'Blessed be He who did not make me a woman'; 'Blessed be He who did not make me an uneducated man.'" (Tosephta, *Berakoth* 7.18)

These references – and they could be multiplied – highlight the great gap that opened up between the godly attitudes conveyed to us in Scripture, and the Jewish society which developed between the Testaments.

Not the whole picture

These quotations are taken from the reactionary Judaism which emerged in the centuries after Jesus, and may reflect some hardening of the oral tradition that existed in his time. Even these traditions are not universally negative about women. Rabbi Hisda, for example, said, "Daughters are dearer to me than sons" (Babylonian Talmud, *Baba Bathra* 141a). There must surely have been many men like Hisda who dearly loved the women in their lives – their mothers, their sisters, their wives, their daughters. Later rabbinical commentators found the statement so astonishing, however, that they assumed either that his sons were dead, or that his daughters had married eminent scholars!

Other rabbis argued:

"The compassion of God is not as the compassion of men. The compassion of men extends to men more than women, but not thus is the compassion of God; His compassion extends equally to men and women and to all." (*Sifre Numbers* 133.49)

"God does not act thus: all are equal before Him, women, slaves, rich and poor." (*Exodus Rabbah* 21.4)

"Whether it be Israelite or Gentile, man or woman, slave or handmaid, whoever does a good deed shall find the reward at its side." (Yalkut, *Lek leka* 76)

Jewish inscriptions collected from across the Mediterranean world over a long period from the first century before Christ to the sixth century after Christ indicate that in many places women played an active role in synagogue life, with titles such as *Presbutera*, *Mother of the Synagogue*, or even *Hierisa*, 'priestess'.

Representative enough

Even with these important qualifications, however, it is obvious from glimpses in Jesus' parables and several incidents in the gospels that the quotations above are not exceptions, but representative of the way in which many 'teachers of the Law' thought about women. Their negative, contemptuous attitude to women was chauvinism in large phylacteries and long tassels.

Little wonder that the Lord Jesus was several times moved to speak out forcefully against the contempt and abuse evident in his generation: and his sharp rebuke to the twelve rings through time. "Leave her alone! ... Why do you trouble the woman?" (John 12:7; Matthew 26:10). How easily superficial social attitudes infiltrate the family of God!

61

12

THE LORD JESUS AND WOMEN

IT is time to focus on him in whom the living Word of God was made man. Luke has a special interest in Jesus' interactions with women, but each writer tells a consistent story.

Here is the divine man with a profound love and care for the women in his life – mother, friends and disciples, suppliants and sinners. He prioritises spiritual learning and praises faith, but he also cares deeply for their physical and emotional needs. He gladly heals them and those they love. He does not neglect women in his teaching. They are there sweeping the house to find a coin and rejoicing with friends when it is found; obtaining justice by prayerful persistence; grinding at the mill; hiding leaven in some meal. He holds them up as examples of faith, and rebukes those who speak out of self-righteousness and privilege.

His teaching and practice, both personally and through the apostles whom he chose and guided into all truth, must define our own.

"Be it unto me according to thy word"

Christ was not yet conceived when the angel came to Mary with joyful but challenging words: "Behold, you will conceive in your womb and bear a son, and you shall call his name Jesus". Unlike Zacharias, Mary did not ask for a sign but accepted God's plan for her with unhesitating faith. No doubt she brought to mind the divine purpose achieved through Sarah and Manoah's wife, women similarly visited. Perhaps she pondered over this appearance to her alone without Joseph, seeing in it the promise of an almighty Being who would achieve salvation by His own hand, and His hand alone.

Mary would need this and further reassurance in the years that followed, when her son at twelve appeared strangely impractical and insensitive, lost in the Temple and forgetful of his family; or when he left the family home at thirty and distanced himself from her, when he began to draw the great crowds, to live the impossibly busy life, to challenge the authorities in a way which greatly alarmed his family.

Then came the terrible moment when a sword pierced her soul and darkness came over all the earth. But even in the hour of his greatest need he focuses his mind and draws an agonising breath to provide for her. "Woman, behold your son!" These simple words ensured shelter and some solace as he entrusted her to his most loved disciple.

"One thing is needful"

It is Luke who first introduces us to Martha and Mary, the wealthy and well-connected sisters of Bethany (10:38-43). Martha is an ardent supporter of the Lord, and generously invites Jesus and his large party into her home for a meal. The sisters set to work; but at some point, Mary makes a conscious choice to leave her sister's side and seat herself at Jesus' feet. Martha grows more and more resentful, more and more agitated. Eventually the sight is more than she can bear, and she bursts in on Jesus: "Lord, do you not care that my sister has left me to serve alone? Tell her then to help me." Jesus responds with the gentlest of rebukes: "Martha, Martha!" Her generosity and her diligence were good things, and he does not criticize them. But to feast on his words is even more important: in fact, it is "one thing" that is absolutely necessary. Under no circumstances will he be taking away from Mary the opportunity to hear his words with an open heart and a listening ear.

We should not cast Martha superficially as a bustling, insensitive matron, because there is no doubt that she was also a good listener and a great believer. Some time later their beloved Lazarus fell sick. An urgent message was dispatched to Jesus. They watched and waited. Their anxiety intensified as Lazarus grew rapidly worse. Still no help came. Lazarus died. Grieving, they prepared his body and buried him in a rock tomb. Only on the fourth day did Jesus, at last, arrive. The sisters were devastated, but Martha's conviction was unshaken:

"I know that whatever you ask of God, God will give you ... I know that he will rise again in the resurrection on the last day ... I have believed that you are the Christ, the Son of God, even he who comes into the world."   (John 11:22,24,27, NASB)

Her strong faith was powerfully rewarded when she saw the glory of God, and Lazarus coming forth at the Lord's cry of command.

"Thy faith hath saved thee"

The Jewish authorities came to the conclusion that Jesus must be killed for the good of the nation. The time was not ripe for the final collision, and he went away into the wilderness to spend some months with his disciples. When he returned, it was to the house of Simon the leper, where Lazarus sat at table with him, Martha served – and Mary broke open an alabaster bottle and anointed his head with the priceless nard it contained. The Lord was so deeply touched by her unique insight, profound love and uncalculating devotion that he insisted that the preaching of the gospel should be accompanied by the retelling of her story "wheresoever this gospel shall be preached throughout the whole world".

Three gospels obviously complied with his wish (Matthew 26:6-13; Mark 14:3-9; John 12:1-8). But where is Luke? A story in Luke 7:36-50 contains so many similarities that it must be either an earlier equivalent incident involving the same people – Simon, Mary and the Lord – or the same story, recorded by Luke in a different setting for a special reason. Perhaps the former is the more likely. In the next chapter (8:43-48), the woman with a discharge of blood shows similar qualities: the faith to approach, to stand hesitatingly behind him, and bend at his feet, the courage to endure the embarrassment of a problem exposed before all. To both the anointed man responds with words of healing and blessing: "Your faith has made you well; go in peace."

A sharp contrast

But Jesus' concern for these women was typical of the compassion he extended to all women. With the same compassion he reached out and touched the woman of Samaria, delivered a resurrected son to the weeping widow of Nain and a healed daughter to the Syrophoenician woman, released the woman bound by Satan, redeemed the woman caught in adultery, noticed and acclaimed the poor but faithful widow giving her meal-money to God, and gave Mary Magdalene back her Lord. Pray God our attitude to each other shall be like his!

13

HE APPOINTED TWELVE

LITTLE wonder that the Lord chose with great care, after a night of prayer, those who were to "be with him", to preach, and to heal the sick (Mark 3:14,15). Their support and friendship were very important to him; but always in his mind there was the larger role beyond the three hectic years of his ministry. Sometimes they are called apostles, 'those sent', even before his ascension (Matthew 10:2; Mark 6:30; Luke 6:13; 9:10; 11:49; 17:5; 22:14; 24:10); for he intended from the beginning that they should become his authorized representatives.

They were the formal recipients of the Lord's commandments (Acts 1:2). Later they would wield his authority in the ecclesia (Acts 2:14; 5:12,18,40,42; 6:2-4; 9:29; 15:2; Galatians 1:17), accompanied by special powers (Acts 2:43; 5:12; 2 Corinthians 12:12). The teaching of Christ became "the apostles' doctrine", and all who entered the ecclesia were inducted into "the apostles' fellowship" (Acts 2:42; 1 John 1:3) – as indeed we are today. They were responsible for endorsing the early extensions of the gospel (Acts 8:14; 11:1,22). Special honours will be theirs: "You who have followed me will also sit on twelve thrones, judging the twelve tribes of Israel" (Matthew 19:28; Luke 22:30). And their names are inscribed on the foundation stones of the New Jerusalem (Ephesians 2:20; Revelation 21:14).

Little is known about their personal circumstances. Some, perhaps most, were from the towns which nestled between the hills of Galilee and the shores of its lake. Two might have been from different planets: Matthew was a hated tax collector, arrested by Jesus in the middle of his daily work; Simon had previously sworn allegiance to the Zealots, a fanatical Jewish terrorist organization.

Clearly Jesus deliberately chose the marginal and the despised without regard for public opinion. He did not care that people might think his followers uneducated provincials – as they were in fact considered (Acts 4:13). He did not care whether the inclusion of Matthew annoyed or offended any and all patriotic Jews. He did not care whether the inclusion of Simon made the authorities anxious. His choices were controversial. He simply did not care.

Did Jesus simply bow to convention in appointing male apostles?

Then why were no women included in the number – or in the seventy sent to preach on another occasion?* We can surely rule out oversight: so the selection of men only was conscious and deliberate. We have examined the Lord's attitude to women: so we can rule out prejudice. It has been conjectured that Jesus did not choose women because it would not have been culturally appropriate at the time. The conjecture is completely implausible. It ignores the great weight of evidence in the gospels that Jesus was not out to placate, but to challenge his society – a lesson that Christ's disciples should not miss in today's world, obsessed as it is with social and political correctness at the expense of authenticity, a deep relationship with God, true justice and genuine compassion.

Let us make an attempt to assemble the evidence in one place. In Nazareth, his home town, we see Jesus incensing his neighbours in the synagogue by comparing them unfavourably with the people of Sidon and Syria, and pointing out that the absence of any

---

* Though it is impossible to be dogmatic, there is nothing to suggest any women in the band of seventy preachers who were sent on a preaching tour later in the Lord's ministry, either (Luke 10:1ff). "Other" (Luke 10:1) is Greek *eterous*, masculine; "them" is Greek *autous*, also masculine. Masculine pronouns also occur in verses 2 and 7. The limited evidence suggests a company of men.

miracles in their midst was because they refused to accept him as a prophet (Luke 4:23-30). In Jerusalem, we see him not once, but twice, entering the holy Temple and creating mayhem by expelling the merchants and their customers, overturning the trading desks of the money-changers, and the chairs of the bird-sellers, accusing them of making it "a den of thieves" (John 2:13-17; Matthew 21:12,13; Mark 11:15-18; Luke 19:45,46), and apparently threatening to destroy the Temple when challenged (John 2:18-22).

Then we come across him engaging a Samaritan woman in conversation. Even his disciples, used to his unconventional behaviour, raised their eyebrows (John 4:9,27). He touches a leper with his bare hands (Matthew 8:1-4; Mark 1:40-45). He eats and drinks wine with tax-collectors and 'sinners' (Matthew 9:10-13; 11:16-19; Mark 2:15-17; Luke 5:30,31; 7:31-35; 15:1,2; 19:1-10).

We find him repeatedly challenging the accepted formal interpretation of the Sabbath laws, dear to the hearts of pious Jews as one of the distinctives of their religion, by healing, defending the actions of his disciples, even claiming lordship of the day – often in the synagogues under the very noses of the authorities (Matthew 12:1-13; Mark 2:23–3:6; Luke 6:1-11; 13:10-17; 14:1-6; John 5). He taught that the widely accepted application of the divorce laws to any and every cause of dissatisfaction constituted legalized adultery (Matthew 5:31,32; 19:3-9; Mark 10:1-12; Luke 16:17,18). He urged people compelled by a soldier of the deeply resented occupation force to carry his pack one mile, to "go with him two miles" (Matthew 5:41).

He openly praised a centurion's faith as greater than any he had found in Israel (Matthew 8:13; Luke 7:9), and compared the communities of Israel unfavourably with those of Tyre and Sidon, Sodom and Nineveh (Matthew 11:20-24; 12:39-42). He set a Samaritan against a priest and a Levite as a model of neighbourly love for "a certain lawyer" to imitate (Luke 10:25-37), and a publican against a Pharisee as a model of penitence and justification (18:10-14). He repeatedly criticized his generation to their face as "hypocrites", "a wicked and adulterous generation", "faithless and perverse", "fools and blind", "serpents" who would not escape the damnation of hell, including at least one occasion when "the crowds were increasing" (Matthew 16:2-4; 17:17; 22:18; Mark 9:19; Luke 9:41; 11:29; 12:56; 16:14,15; John 4:48).

He trounced "the teacher of Israel" for his ignorance, dullness and unbelief (John 3:1-12). He condemned as evil the "Pharisees and doctors of the law" who questioned his authority to forgive sins (Matthew 9:1-7; Mark 2:1-12; Luke 5:17-26). He taught that the righteousness of the scribes and Pharisees was inadequate (Matthew 5:20). He condemned as hypocritical public almsgiving, penitence and prayer (Matthew 6:1-18). He castigated the Jewish leaders for substituting their own traditions for the Word of God, condemned the practice of *korban*, and set aside the significance of ritual washings (Matthew 15:1-14; Mark 7:1-23). On more than one occasion, he took his host to task (Luke 7:36-50; 11:37-54; 14:12-14). He informed the chief priests and the elders that the publicans and the harlots would enter the kingdom of God before them (Matthew 21:28-32). He rebuked the Sadducees for their ignorance of the Scriptures and their Author (Matthew 22:29-32; Mark 12:24). He publicly criticised the teachings and practices of the Pharisees in the hearing of the multitude (Matthew 23:1-33; Mark 12:38-40; Luke 20:45-47). He told the Jewish leaders, among other things, that neither the Word of God nor the love of God was in them (John 5:38,42), that they preferred human praise to "the glory that comes from the only God" (5:44), that they did not believe the writings of Moses (5:45-47), that they would have to eat his flesh and drink his blood if they were to have life (6:53), that they did not keep the law (7:19), that they judged after the flesh (8:15), that they would die in their sins (8:21,24; 9:41), that their father was the devil, and that they obeyed his sinful impulses (8:44), and that they were liars (8:55).*

These are hardly the words or actions of a man who cared for what was culturally appropriate! "I have not come to bring peace, but a sword", he said (Matthew 10:34). "I came to cast fire on the earth", he said (Luke 12:49). Was it not precisely because he represented such a tremendous challenge to his society that the establishment arrested him, condemned him on the basis of trumped up charges and false testimony, and had him crucified?

So the selection by Jesus of a small band of "men and brothers" to be his authorized representatives on the earth was neither an oversight, nor a sign of prejudice, nor a concession to convention, but a deliberate decision in line with the established Scriptural pattern of male responsibility.

The pattern carried forward by the apostles

And the apostles consistently carried the pattern forward. When it came time to choose a replacement for Judas, Peter "stood up among the brothers", and put the case that "one of these men ... must become with us a witness to his resurrection" (Acts 1:22).

Three significant words are used of humans in the Greek New Testament. The most common, *anthropos*, occurs a little more than 500 times, and refers to human beings, male and female. *Gune* occurs more than 220 times, and always refers to females, often in the special sense of 'wife'. *Aner* occurs about 200 times, and always refers to men, often in the special sense of 'husband'. Although the word does not always carry the strong sense 'male', it is never used directly of women.

---

* Two counter-examples should be noted. The first is Jesus' frequent practice when healing the profoundly diseased, particularly those affected by mental illness, of accepting, apparently, the existence of demons. The second is the miracle of the taxation coins (Matthew 17:24-27). Neither supplies a parallel for Jesus' choice only of men as apostles.

It is this word that Peter uses, making it clear that only a male could qualify as an apostle.

Yet the women in that room were in fact highly qualified to be witnesses of the resurrection. As Jesus had travelled from village to village showing the glad tidings of the kingdom of God, there were with him "certain women, which had been healed of evil spirits and infirmities, Mary called Magdalene, out of whom went seven devils, and Joanna the wife of Chuza Herod's steward, and Susanna, and many others, which ministered unto him of their substance" (Luke 8:2,3). It was a beautiful example of gratitude for blessings received, and of the willingness of each woman to do "what she could" by providing personal care for Jesus as he proclaimed the gospel.

These same women were with him to "the end", horror-stricken witnesses to his death agony, followers of the small, sad funeral procession that made its way to the rock tomb nearby, silent watchers as the body was laid to rest. When the Sabbath was over, some of them rose before dawn and headed for the tomb to anoint their Lord's body, concerned perhaps that only the briefest of attentions had been possible before the onset of the Passover (Matthew 27:55,56,61; 28:1; Mark 15:40,41,47; 16:1,2; Luke 23:49,55,56; 24:1,2; John 19:25-27; 20:1-18). To them Jesus revealed himself first, in the garden and on the road back to Jerusalem, commissioning them to carry to the twelve the joyful news that he was risen, and that they should meet him in Galilee, as arranged.

In Jewish society of the time, women were not accepted as witnesses in court, except in a few rare cases, such as the death of a husband or the unfaithfulness of another woman. Women were considered prone to lying (*Yalqut Shimeoni* 1.82). Josephus urged, "Let not the testimony of women be admitted, on account of the levity and boldness of their sex" (*Antiquities of the Jews* 4.219). And the Talmud also insisted that witnesses should be men, not women or minors (*Yoma* 43).

So the women were not believed – as Jesus no doubt knew would happen! "These words seemed to them an idle tale, and they did not believe them" (Luke 24:11). "Some women of our company amazed us", the pair on the road to Emmaus told the incognito Jesus, "They were at the tomb early in the morning, and when they did not find his body, they came back saying that they had even seen a vision of angels, who said that he was alive. Some of those who were with us went to the tomb and found it just as the women had said, but him they did not see" (24:22-24).

But within a few hours the apostles knew that the women had spoken the truth. It is interesting to note that in the first roll of the Jerusalem ecclesia "the women" are next noted after the apostles (Acts 1:14). The twelve had learned a new respect for these faithful witnesses.

Yet only two candidates were nominated to replace Judas. Both were men. And when 'the lot fell on Matthias', it was clear that the Lord had made his choice known. When it came time to add a special emissary to the Gentiles, Paul was added, "as to one untimely born"; again, a man (Romans 11:13; 1 Corinthians 15:8).

Other apostles

Were others known as apostles? There is limited evidence of that. Barnabas and Paul are called "the apostles" when preaching together in Iconium (Acts 14:4,14), but Barnabas is not referred to as an apostle on any other occasion, even when with Paul (for example, 15:2,12,22,25,35). Silas and Timothy are implicitly included with Paul in the same way (1 Thessalonians 2:6). As with Barnabas, however, they are never called apostles on any other occasion. James the brother of Jesus is also grouped with the apostles (Galatians 1:19).

There is one other relevant passage, and that is the intriguing reference by Paul to "Andronicus and Junia, my kinsmen, and my fellow prisoners. They are well known to the apostles, and they were in Christ before me" (Romans 16:7). Who were these two Jewish Christians in Rome? And were they also apostles?

Although there is some debate among scholars about whether Greek *Iounian* refers to a woman or a man, the current majority view is that it should be translated 'Junia', and Junia would therefore be a sister in Christ. It is possible that Andronicus and Junia were a married couple, but we really know nothing of them. All we can say is that they were longtime disciples who had once shared a cell with Paul.

Then what of his description of them as being "well known to the apostles"? He could mean that they were "notable apostles"; or he could mean that they were "well regarded by the apostles"? Both are possible grammatically: we cannot be certain what Paul intended. If Paul did in fact mean that they were "notable apostles", then in what sense? The term "apostle" is twice used in a lesser sense of official ecclesial messengers (2 Corinthians 8:23; Philippians 2:25), and once in a general sense, "he that is sent" (John 13:16). If the description "apostle" is intended to apply to this faithful couple, perhaps it is in this more general sense.

Aside from these references, the term "the apostles" is always reserved for the twelve, and Paul. And as we have seen, first the Lord Jesus, then the apostles consciously and deliberately chose only brethren for this role, even though qualified sisters were available. It was neither oversight, nor prejudice, nor cultural accommodation; but a continuing application of the principle of male responsibility which began in Eden. And the same consistent approach was taken to other leadership roles in the first century ecclesia, as we shall see.

14

A CONSISTENT PATTERN IN LEADERSHIP

THE apostles could not be everywhere, or see to everything. As the Jerusalem Ecclesia grew, under the grace of God, beyond its original 120 members, a group of leaders emerged to support the apostles. And as the gospel spread far and wide, into Syria, and North Africa, Asia, Greece and Italy, a leadership framework was needed in each local ecclesia.

Guided by the Spirit of God, the apostles found their model in the community governance that characterised village life in Israel. The old heads, 'the elders', with a wealth of experience, having absorbed the Word of God and reflected on its meaning over a lifetime, were the custodians of Israel's heritage. They would gather at the village gate to make arrangements for the good of the community as a whole, to decide difficult questions, to witness transactions.

In Israel's past the arrangement had frequently broken down. In the days of the judges the elders appear lost, pragmatic rather than spiritual, cynical rather than faithful. In the days of the prophets the elders sometimes led the people in responding to prophetic warnings and exhortations, and sometimes led the persecution of God's messengers. In Jesus' day the elders saw him as a radical challenge to their authority, the tradition of which they were the stewards, and the stability of the nation. They gathered with the Pharisees, the scribes and lawyers, and the priests, to arrange his betrayal, arrest, condemnation and execution. After his resurrection they persisted in attacking his followers right through the Acts record. Old men are not always wise, or godly.

Elders and bishops

So it was not satisfactory for the ecclesia to be governed simply by its oldest members. They must also be godly, faithful and holy men, spiritually alert, sound, hospitable, competent to teach, loving, patient, moderate and even-tempered, beyond corruption, well regarded in the community, with households that were a tribute to their godly leadership. Typical criteria are set out in the Pastoral Letters (1 Timothy 3:1-7; Titus 1:5-9). A council of these men, guided by the Word of God in the mouth of the apostles, provided the ideal leadership for an infant ecclesia.

This arrangement is first mentioned in Acts, where the elders of the Jerusalem ecclesia received the donation of the Antioch ecclesia at the hand of Paul and Barnabas (Acts 11:30). The same elders gathered with the apostles and the body of brothers and sisters to decide the circumcision question at the Council of Jerusalem (15:2,4,6,22,23; 16:4), and again to receive Paul's report and the Jerusalem Poor Fund (21:18-20).

But the practice of ordaining elders was extended to Gentile ecclesias also, as appears from Paul's first great missionary journey (14:22,23). Having reached Derbe, Paul and Barnabas retraced their steps, consolidating the disciples, exhorting them, cautioning them about the tribulation that would come to them, praying with them – and ordaining elders in each local ecclesia. The Ephesus ecclesia had elders, whom Paul summoned to Miletus for his farewell address (21:17). As we learn from his brief to Titus, it was Paul's practice to ordain elders in every city (Titus 1:5).

The Greek *presbuteros* is a comparative, and sometimes refers literally to an older man, or in its feminine form to an older woman. On almost all occasions, however, it is used in a technical sense of those responsible for the governance of the ecclesia. The Greek *episkopos*, 'bishop, overseer' is an alternative description – although the meaning is different, it refers to the same group of people (Acts 20:17, cp. 20:28; Titus 1:5, cp. 1:7; 1 Peter 5:1,5, cp. 5:2).*

Elder-overseers were responsible for the spiritual health of the members (James 5:14, cp. Hebrews 12:15). The shepherd was the model for their work (Acts 20:28; 1 Peter 5:1-5): they were to be shepherds and overseers in the mould of the Lord Christ (2:25). They were to be treated with respect and affection (1 Thessalonians 5:12,13; 1 Timothy 5:1), particularly those who dedicated themselves to teaching and preaching (5:17), and their integrity was to be challenged only if independent witnesses could vouch for a serious misdemeanour (verse 19). They were also responsible for sponsoring and confirming the appointment of ecclesial servants (4:14). The apostles were pleased to refer to themselves as bishops and elders (Acts 1:20; 1 Peter 5:1, cp. 2 John 1; 3 John 1). In the book of Revelation they are pictured sitting about the throne (4:4; 5:6; 7:11), leading the redeemed in devotion and worship (4:10; 5:8,11,14; 11:16; 14:3; 19:4), and assisting John to understand the meaning of the prophecy as it is unfolded – an interesting illustration of the requirement that elders should be "apt to teach" (5:5; 7:13).

A male role

Today's 'Arranging Committee' and 'Arranging Brethren' is a general approximation of the body of elders, although they have not been ordained by the apostles or their representatives, and do not possess miraculous Spirit-gifts. Despite these significant differences their responsibilities in the local ecclesia are broadly similar to those of their first century counterparts, and the same spiritual qualities are

---

* References to those who "lead" or "rule over" are found in Acts 15:22; Romans 12:8; 1 Thessalonians 5:12; 1 Timothy 5:17, cp. 1 Timothy 3:4,5,12 and Hebrews 13:7,17,24. The terms should not be pushed too far, but certainly indicate leadership by example, and suggest some authority, to which the "younger", and the ecclesia generally, were called upon to submit.

surely required in those deemed suitable for the responsibility.

There is no hint in Scripture that sisters, even aged sisters with extensive life experience and having great spiritual wisdom, were at any time appointed or ordained as elder-overseers. They did not lack the skills or the spiritual qualifications. Scripture yields the names of many faithful and highly competent sisters, and there are very many among us today. Their spiritual and practical thoughts, their recommendations, their godly counsel and wise advice are highly prized, closely listened to, carefully considered. But God has consistently imposed the final responsibility for leading His people on the shoulders of His sons.

The Lord Jesus chose brothers to be apostles, chose another brother to plug the gap, added another brother when the work of ecclesia-building had to begin in earnest among the Gentiles. The apostles chose only brothers to oversee and lead local ecclesias.

Scripture knows only this model: "I do not permit a woman to teach or to exercise authority over a man", said Paul, very directly (1 Timothy 2:12). The statement is clearly in line with his teaching and practice at other times and in other places; and it is also consistent with the Bible's approach more generally. If we are genuinely endeavouring to build the living house of the ecclesia on the foundation of the Lord, his apostles and prophets, if we are sincere about patterning ourselves on the example of the first century ecclesia – then this is our model. The alternatives have neither apostolic teaching nor apostolic practice to commend them. They are not of God.

15

SERVICE

THE same principles are evident in another role – that of deacons. The introduction of deacons was also triggered by the growth of the ecclesia beyond its original 120 members. Not only did the Jerusalem ecclesia grow larger: it also became more diverse. A large number of Greek-speaking Jews joined their Palestinian brothers and sisters; and a problem emerged.

The ecclesia numbered more than 8,000 members – perhaps as many as 10,000. Although the Acts record speaks of "the full number of the disciples", it appears that their size made it impractical to meet in one place; and ecclesial meetings were therefore conducted house to house in small groups (Acts 2:46; 5:42; 12:12). The groups naturally formed around existing networks, based on family relationships, personal friendships, and cultural links. Every day, welfare – "the daily distribution" (Greek, *diakonia*) – was made through the same networks to the poor brothers and sisters who were excluded from the extensive Jewish social support system because of their faith. It became apparent that the widows among the Greek-speaking Jews, at the cultural margins of the ecclesia, were being overlooked. Trouble began to brew.

The apostles became aware of the problem, and called the ecclesia together. They agreed that it was important, but again, they could not be everywhere, or do everything. In any case prayer, and the ministry (Greek, *diakonia*) of the word – that is, the preaching of the gospel – must be their highest priorities.

The apostles proposed another solution. Let the ecclesia choose seven men with the right spiritual credentials to oversee the administration of welfare (Acts 6:3). And "men" is what they meant: the Greek *aner* is used, and as we have seen, that implies 'males', not simply 'humans'. Why not sisters? After all, it was sisters, widows, who were being overlooked. Were the sisters less capable? Did they lack the necessary skills in financial administration, or in care giving? Were they less able to assess, calculate and provide for the daily food and clothing requirements of poor households? The answer to these questions must be, 'No'. Sisters have all these skills, and no doubt they carried out much of the work using these very skills. But the seven were to be "appointed over" the business. They had an oversight role: and the apostles, in line with the principle of male responsibility evident in their own selection by the Lord Jesus, decided that brothers, suitably qualified, should oversee the serving (Greek, *diakoneo*) of tables.

This innovation was a great success, and Luke immediately notes that "the word of God continued to increase, and the number of the disciples multiplied greatly in Jerusalem" (Acts 6:7).

A lasting innovation

The apostles were addressing a specific practical need: and there was probably little thought at the time of extending the new role they had created – the ecclesial servant, or deacon (Greek, *diakonos*).* But as the apostles and their fellows took the gospel into all the world, they took the concept of the deacon with them; and it became a distinct role within the broader framework of ecclesial administration (cp. Philippians 1:1). Spiritual credentials continued to be important,

---

* It should be noted that the family of Greek words – *diakoneo, diakonia, diakonos* – does not always bear the technical meaning of "appointed ecclesial servant". In the apostolic writings the terms are also used of government officials (Romans 13:4, twice), of the work of Christ (Romans 15:8; Galatians 2:17), of angels (Hebrews 1:14) and of the prophets (1 Peter 1:12). But 64 out of 70 references in the apostolic writings are to appointed ecclesial servants and ecclesial service.

and those who had not demonstrated their spiritual commitment and maturity both in their own lives and in the leadership of their families were not considered ready to serve as deacons, whatever their innate skills (1 Timothy 3:8-13).

Some deacons carried on the original work, overseeing the distribution of welfare to needy brothers and sisters. "Relief" (Greek, *diakonia*) was sent from Antioch to Jerusalem (Acts 11:29; 12:25), the catalyst for the great Jerusalem Poor Fund. Later, Paul was pleased to describe himself as the deacon of the Greek ecclesias, delivering the Poor Fund to their brothers and sisters in Jerusalem (Romans 15:25,31; 2 Corinthians 8:4,19,20; 9:1,12,13). It is also used in this sense in his letter to the Romans: "Having gifts that differ according to the grace given to us, let us use them" (Romans 12:7, twice).

But the terms expanded to cover a whole category of ecclesial responsibility, "varieties of service" (1 Corinthians 12:5; 16:15; Ephesians 4:12; Hebrews 6:10, twice; 1 Peter 4:10,11; Revelation 2:19), including teaching and exhortation (1 Timothy 4:6), preaching (2 Timothy 4:5), and personal assistance to the apostles (Acts 19:22; Ephesians 6:21; Colossians 1:7; 4:7,17; 1 Thessalonians 3:2; 2 Timothy 1:18; 4:5,11; Philemon 13). They are even used, early on, of the apostles and their work (Acts 1:17,25). In fact, Paul uses them frequently of himself, and the various contexts suggest that when he wished to play down the authority of his apostleship, and simply state the fact of service, these were the terms he preferred (Acts 20:24; 21:19; 1 Corinthians 3:5; 2 Corinthians 3:3,6,7,8, 9(twice); 4:1; 5:18; 6:3,4; 11:8, 15(twice),23; Ephesians 3:7; Colossians 1:23,25; 1 Timothy 1:12; and note especially Romans 11:13) – an insight into the deeply genuine humility of that great servant of the Lord.*

---

* In 2 Corinthians, no doubt, Paul was also using the word to support his case that the Corinthians should support the great *diakonia*, the Jerusalem Poor Fund. The case is built carefully, and he comes explicitly to the Fund only in chapters 8–9.

Sisters who serve

It is important to note that, while the majority of references are to male deacons, sisters also served as deacons.

Some expositors have taken 1 Timothy 3:11 as a reference to sister-deacons, but there is no objective evidence to support that understanding of the passage. Verses 12,13 clearly speak of male deacons, and verses 9,10 use male terms. The point is that, as in verses 4,5 and Titus 1:6,8, the character of a deacon's wife and children must accord with his own commitment to godly living.

Consider the opposite case. If his children were out of control and his wife outrageous, gossipy, dishonest and loose – then *prima facie* something is seriously wrong in that house, which reflects first and foremost on the character of the deacon, as its God-appointed head. Faithfulness begins at home. If there are obvious problems, they should be addressed before significant ecclesial responsibility is considered.

But other passages do speak of sister-deacons. Phoebe, a deacon of the ecclesia in the port of Cenchrea, near Corinth, was entrusted with the highly responsible task of carrying Paul's letter to Rome (Romans 16:1). It is probable that here, as in nearly every other place, the term should be understood to refer to an ecclesial appointment. Other Greek words are also used of sisters who are named as ecclesial servants (Romans 16:3,12; Philippians 4:3; 1 Timothy 5:9,10).

This underscores the fact that, aside from the teaching and governance of the ecclesia as a whole, which the apostles specifically reserved for qualified brothers, ecclesias should choose the best members for the job, whether male or female. This is God's intention in blessing the ecclesia with a diversity of people and gifts.

Consistent with these principles, almost all ecclesial service is open to both brothers and sisters, and we should appoint those whom God has gifted with the aptitude and skills to serve His ecclesia effectively, whether male or female.

16

PROPHECY

HAVING examined the pattern set by the Lord Jesus Christ in choosing his apostles, a pattern followed by the apostles in choosing elders, we turn to two significant Spirit-gifts, and examine the policy and practice of the apostles with respect to prophecy and teaching. We would expect to see the same Scriptural logic at work: and indeed we do.

What do we mean by prophecy? While we tend to associate prophecy with the spectacularly accurate forecasts of the future which only God can communicate, it has a broader sense of "inspired speech", whether God's words of encouragement, rebuke or challenge to His people, or His declaration of the future.

Critically important and highly desirable

Prophecy, therefore, passing directly from God to the first Christians through the prophets, channelled the spoken will of God for the young ecclesias, and was a critically important work of the Comforter, especially before the inspired documents of the New Testament began to be copied and circulated. Prophets are next mentioned after apostles in Paul's lists of the gifts (1 Corinthians 12:28,29; Ephesians 4:11).* Prophets are paired with apostles both by Jesus (Luke 11:49), Paul

---

* An earlier listing (1 Corinthians 12:8-10) is in a different order. The point here is 'unity in diversity', and no point is being made about the order of the gifts. It may be that Paul deliberately begins with "the word of wisdom", "the word of knowledge", and "faith", which do not occur in other lists of Spirit-gifts, to encourage the Corinthians to think more widely about how God works – not always through the obviously spectacular and miraculous.

(Ephesians 2:20; 3:5), Peter (2 Peter 3:2) and John (Revelation 19:20), which underlines their authority and importance. With the apostles, they laid the foundation for the household of God in the first century. Today, our responsibility is to build on their foundational work.

Prophecy was highly desirable because it brought many benefits to the congregation, confirming them in their faith, building them up, rebuking and encouraging them, giving them strength and urging them on (Acts 15:32; 1 Corinthians 14:1,ff.). Prophets could read minds and hearts, convicting those who came into their presence of sin, of righteousness and of judgment, inducing worship and a powerful certainty (14:22-25, cp. Acts 5:1-11).

The identical gift in Old and New Testaments

There is no reason to think, as some have argued, that the gift of prophecy in New Testament times was different from the gift in Old Testament times. There are many references to Old and New Testament prophets in the New Testament documents. The references are intertwined, exactly the same words are used, and no distinction is ever made.

And the gift appears to have worked in exactly the same way. The prophets shared the same impetus as their Old Testament fellows: they were "moved by the Holy Spirit" (2 Peter 1:19-21). Brothers and sisters could not prophesy simply because they chose to. With other spiritual gifts, prophecy had to be "coveted" and "desired" (1 Corinthians 12:31; 14:1,39). God might give the gift in response to passionate prayer out of a pure heart. Then again, He might not. God gave gifts as and when and to whom it pleased Him for the good of the whole, and for no other purpose. The gifts were not opportunities to be grasped for self-expression and self-fulfilment. They were given by God for Christ-service.

The fact that prophets could regulate their prophesying is also both an Old Testament and a New Testament phenomenon. Jeremiah, frustrated with the continual resistance to this message, and the harassment and persecution that followed, actively suppressed his calling to prophesy, although it burned like a fire inside him, and flared again (Jeremiah 19:9).* There is another example of an unnamed prophet cutting off his words to Amaziah because, "as he was speaking to him", the king made it clear that he was not willing to hear God's counsel (2 Chronicles 25:14-16). Paul likewise insists that "the spirits of prophets are subject to prophets" (1 Corinthians14:32). They could speak only the words they were given from God, but they were able to control when and where they spoke, and for how long. Hence Paul instructs that only two or three should speak, one after the other, and that the other prophets present should bring their gift to bear on the question of authenticity, weighing and endorsing what had been spoken. Should God give a new prophecy on the spot, that was a sure sign of a pressing need, and all other arrangements were to give way to the urgent new message.

The New Testament prophets would also suffer the same vicious persecution as their Old Testament colleagues. The way in which Jesus spoke of "the prophets, and wise men, and scribes" that he would send to the Jewish people indicates that in his mind they stood directly in the line of the Old Testament prophets (Matthew 23:27-39; Luke 6:23; 11:47-51; 24:34,35). Stephen was the first to follow his Master: his stoning followed immediately upon his allusion to Jesus' testimony against Jerusalem, "the city that kills the prophets and stones those who are sent to it!" (Acts 7:52). It was for the blood of all the prophets, Old

---

* There appears to be a gap in his prophecy (1:2,3), which could be as long as 22 years, from the thirteenth year of Josiah, who reigned 31 years (2 Chronicles 34:1), to "the beginning of the reign of Jehoiakim" (Jeremiah 26:1; 27:1), perhaps as late as his fourth year (25:1; 36:1; 45:1, cp. 28:1). Jeremiah's lamentation over the death of Josiah during this apparent period of silence is remarked on in the Chronicles record (2 Chronicles 35:25), but there is no reference to it in the compilation of Jeremiah's prophecies that bears his name.

Testament and New Testament alike, that Jerusalem would be held accountable.

Regrettably, there were even to be Christian "false prophets" or pseudo-prophets, as there had been Hebrew false prophets; and again the same Greek word is used of both (cp. Matthew 7:15; 24:11,24; Mark 13:22; Luke 6:26; 2 Peter 2:1; 1 John 4:1; Revelation 16:13; 19:20; 20:10). Even in this disappointing detail the pattern of the Old Testament continues in the New.

The authority of the prophets

There can be no doubt, therefore, that the prophets who channelled the living word of God to the New Testament ecclesias were exact counterparts of their Old Testament predecessors: and any suggestion that the prophets of the New Testament were less inspired or authoritative than the prophets of the Old is incorrect.

Certainly, prophecies had to be judged (1 Corinthians 14:29) or "proved" (1 Thessalonians 5:21), and the gift of "discerning of spirits" was for precisely that purpose (1 Corinthians 12:10). That was because, as John explained, "many false prophets have gone out into the world" (1 John 4:1). Therefore it was necessary to "try the spirits whether they are of God". "Not even the preaching of an apostle was credited unaccompanied by scriptural investigation."* For the same reason Paul expected the prophets of Corinth to recognise and endorse his authoritative apostolic ruling on the way in which the gifts were to be used (1 Corinthians 14:37,38). But the fact that discrimination was needed between the authentic article and the fake does not affect the authority of the true prophets.

The prophets channelled the words of God. They were to add nothing, to subtract nothing, to change nothing (cp. Revelation 22:18,19). That does not mean that the person was irrelevant. As with the writing of the Scriptures, God chose those who were most suitable

---

* An observation on Acts 17:10-12 – John Thomas, *Elpis Israel*, 15th Ed., page 6.

for the work. The prophet or prophetess brought his or her relationship with God to the work of prophecy, his or her faith, passion for God, love of His people, maturity, integrity and humility, all of which were vital to carrying out the task powerfully and fruitfully. But none of the content was human. The words were the words of God, breathed out by Him, a Divine wind impelling the prophets. Hence Paul could insist that the spiritually gifted in Corinth, and especially the prophets, recognise that what he had written to them was not his opinion, or interpretation, or viewpoint, or perspective, or recommendation – but "a command of the Lord" (1 Corinthians 14:37). And he could add, dogmatically, "If anyone does not recognize this, he is not recognized" (verse 38). Such was his inspired authority then: and being "the word of the Lord", it is undiminished by time, and more durable than the fabric of heaven and earth.

The single incident that is sometimes argued against the authority of the Word of God in the mouth of the prophets is the refusal of Paul to be diverted from his mission to Jerusalem by the repeated witness of the Holy Spirit through the prophets "in every city" to the fact that "imprisonment and afflictions" awaited him at his destination (Acts 20:22-24; 21:10-14). But was Paul setting the word of the prophets aside? Indeed, no! The prophecies never urged him to turn back: they only warned him of what lay ahead. It was open to him to believe or disbelieve the string of warnings, and to respond by turning back or by proceeding. He accepted the prophecies, "nothing doubting", and determined to press ahead. Those with him eventually accepted that his resolute faith was indeed the right response, and when they themselves had come to Paul's frame of mind they endorsed it, "saying, The will of the Lord be done". The incident illustrates the fact that we must first rightly understand "the word of the Lord", then respond to it by wholeheartedly doing "the will of the Lord". Only this combination of faith and faith-in-action will draw the Master's praise.

The prophetesses

As with prophets, so prophetesses are both an Old and a New Testament phenomenon. Miriam was a prophetess (Exodus 15:20). So were Deborah (Judges 4:4), Huldah (2 Kings 22:14; 2 Chronicles 34:22) and Anna (Luke 2:36). Lemuel's mother (Proverbs 31:1,ff.) and Isaiah's unnamed wife (Isaiah 8:3) may also be added to the list.

"When the day of Pentecost arrived", the Lord Jesus anointed each member of the ecclesia, male and female, with the Holy Spirit (Acts 2:3,4,33). Peter announced that this was a fulfilment of the prophecy of Joel that God would pour out His Spirit on His sons and His daughters, His servants and His handmaidens (Acts 2:16-18, cp. Joel 2:28-32). Prophetesses are not prominent in the New Testament, but they are certainly there. Philip the evangelist had four daughters who prophesied at Caesarea (Acts 21:9). We read of prophetesses in Corinth (1 Corinthians 11:5,6,13), and it is reasonable to assume that they were active in other ecclesias also.

As there were false prophets, there were also, sadly, false prophetesses who prophesied "out of their own heart" (Ezekiel 13:17-23). Was "the prophetess Noadiah" (Nehemiah 6:14) in that category, or had she lent her genuine gift to the devious purposes of Nehemiah's enemies? The possession of the gift of prophecy did not guarantee right thinking or right living. To obey the Word of God has always been a personal choice, as challenging and critical for the Spirit-inspired as for those who do not possess miraculous gifts.

The character of "Jezebel", on the other hand, is plain (Revelation 2:18-23). Whether this was her real name, or a revealing pseudonym given her by the Lord Jesus, we do not know. But he does not describe her as a prophetess gone off the rails. Rather, he says that she "calls herself a prophetess", which suggests that she had illegitimately claimed the gift, and the authority that went with it. She is condemned for teaching and seducing members of the ecclesia "to practice sexual immorality and to eat food sacrificed to idols", for sexual and spiritual promiscuity; and the elders of the ecclesia at Thyatira, who are otherwise highly commended for their works, their love, their service, their faith, their patience, their selflessness and their humility, are criticised for "suffering" her, for tolerating or accommodating her teaching and her behaviour.

"Praying and prophesying"

In 1 Corinthians 11 prophesying is linked to praying, once in relation to brothers (verse 4), once in relation to sisters (verse 5; and again in verse 13). The link to prophecy suggests two things. First, the praying referred to is probably the act of leading in prayer, not the act of participating passively in communal prayer. Second, the praying referred to may have been a miraculous Spirit-gift like prophecy: and in fact, Paul makes reference to just such a gift in chapter 14.

The gift of foreign languages, or "tongues", was primarily for the proclamation of the gospel in other languages. It was aimed at unbelievers (14:22) who spoke "barbarian" languages; that is, languages other than Greek, the epitome of culture – or so Greeks thought (14:11)! The exercise of the gift in the absence of an interpreter would be spiritually uplifting (14:14,28), but tongues-speakers were none the wiser, as they could not understand what they were saying unless they had also received the gift of interpretation (14:13).

The gift was exercised in a number of ways. Most commonly Paul writes of speaking with tongues (12:30; 13:1; 14:2,4-6,9-13,18,19,21-23,27,28), but he also speaks of praying with tongues (14:14,15), singing with tongues (14:15), and blessing or giving thanks with tongues (14:16,17). As with prophecy, it appears that the words were provided by God. Certainly the tongues speaker had no idea what he or she was saying unless they or another interpreted their words into Greek. The tongues-speaker appears to have played no role in framing the ideas expressed or the words in which they were expressed.

The link between prophesying and praying in chapter 11 suggests that the praying referred to in that chapter should be understood in this miraculous sense.

An enduring work on which we are to build

So that is the New Testament experience of prophecy. Is this miraculous gift active today? Like the gifts of tongues and "the word of knowledge" (cp. 1 Corinthians 12:8) it was given for a time only, and it was "in part". The insights into the mind and will of God were marvellous indeed, but they were disbursed in a limited and fragmentary way to many congregations. Paul foresaw that the time would come when they would pass away, to be replaced by "that which is perfect", "the unity of the faith and of the knowledge of the Son of God ... the measure of the stature of the fulness of Christ" (Ephesians 4:11-16; cp. 1 Corinthians 13:8-13).

The completion of the word of God would bring together all that God had revealed for the shared faith and life of His people, all that was necessary for the transformation of the ecclesia into one body growing up into its head in love, "the perfect man". Absolute perfection will come only in the Kingdom of God: but the ecclesia can attain spiritual maturity in measure as it stands under Christ, answers to him, grows up into him. Even when the Spirit gifts were active, it was "faith, hope, love, these three", greater than any miraculous gifts, which powered this spiritual transformation.

True to Paul's prediction, the gift of prophecy did pass away. Although on rare occasions God had bestowed the gifts directly, on the whole ecclesia at Pentecost, on the household of Cornelius (Acts 10:44-47; 11:15-17), and perhaps also on Paul (9:17), the gifts were generally given only by the laying on of the apostles' hands (for example, 8:14-24; 19:6; 2 Timothy 1:6). When the last apostle died – often thought to be

John, some time after AD 100 – the mechanism for bestowing more gifts ceased. It is interesting that the canon of Scripture was completed by John with the book of Revelation, received and written down in AD 96 according to most commentators, not long before his death.

There is, therefore, no miraculous gift of prophecy today: and in light of the fact that it consisted in channelling God's own words, it would be presumptuous of any person to claim such a gift. Certainly the effects of prophecy continue. Public addresses and private communications should be for "upbuilding and encouragement and consolation" (1 Corinthians 14:3). And the spirit of prophecy continues – "the testimony of Jesus" (Revelation 19:10), a witness to which every disciple contributes in word and deed. But as the role of the apostle had its critical time, and is no longer, the role of the prophet or prophetess is not extant today.

The work of the apostles and prophets lives on in the living house which is built upon the foundation they laid, Jesus Christ, and the living Word of God which presents him to us, no longer spoken and fragmentary but written and complete. It is on that foundation we build today.

17

TEACHING

NOW we turn to the work of teaching. Prophecy and teaching are closely related, but there is a very important difference. The example of Timothy illustrates (2 Timothy 3:14-17).

Timothy had been taught by his grandmother Lois and his mother Eunice. Paul had no doubt built on this early instruction. Timothy was exhorted by Paul, "Continue thou in the things which thou hast learned and hast been assured of, knowing of whom thou hast learned them". How had Timothy been taught? From the Scriptures, which he had known "from childhood". The Scriptures had been breathed out by God, and written down by "holy men of God". But the process did not stop there. The teacher stepped in, applying the Scriptures profitably for the purposes of "teaching" or "systematic instruction", "for reproof, for correction, and for training in righteousness".

The difference between the prophet and the teacher becomes apparent. The revelation of the Word of God, which would become Scripture as it was written down, was the work of the prophet. The authority of the prophets and prophetesses lay with God: for the words they spoke were God's words. The teachers drew on a range of sources – the Hebrew Scriptures and the developing collection of Greek Scriptures, together "God's Word written"; prophetic utterances; and the oral history of apostolic teaching and practice – to systematically instruct the ecclesias in the content of Scripture, to refute wrong ideas, to correct moral faults, and to apply Scripture to the practical questions of righteous living. Like the prophets, the authority of the teachers lay with the Scriptures from which they taught: by contrast to the prophets, all the words were the teacher's own.

Of course, the teacher must stick close to the Scriptures, must be a conscientious and careful artisan, "rightly handling the word of truth" (2 Timothy 2:15). Nevertheless, while the inspired Scriptures were the basis and substance of the teacher's work, the choice of theme and content, the emphasis, the application, the words themselves – all lay with the teacher. Hence, the ecclesia is never said to be built on the foundation of the first century teachers, but on the foundation of the apostles and prophets, who spoke for God and represented the living Christ with authority.

A crucial work

Despite this significant difference, however, there is no question about the critical importance of teaching work, and teachers are often mentioned alongside or next after prophets (Acts 11:26; 13:1; 1 Corinthians 12:28,29; 14:6; Ephesians 4:11).

Teaching was initially the work of the apostles (Acts 2:42), who preached by teaching (cp. 4:2,18; 5:21,25,28,42; 13:12; 15:35; 17:19; 18:11; 20:20; 28:31; Colossians 1:28; 2:7; 1 Timothy 2:7), opening up the Old Testament Scriptures to their Jewish audience and showing them their true meaning – that in all the Scriptures Jesus Christ the Son of God is held out as the key to God's purpose with mankind. They combined teaching with proclamation of the fact of Christ's resurrection and the certainty of his coming again in power and great glory to raise the dead, judge the world in righteousness, and establish the Kingdom of God: and these continue to be the twin tasks of preaching today.

There are many references to teachers and teaching in the New Testament, but in most cases it is not possible to distinguish between Spirit-gifted and other teaching activity. Perhaps the difference was not very important. Some gifts, such as apostleship and prophecy, could only be of God. But the gift of tongues, for example, provided a miraculous capacity to speak foreign languages which dedicated students could develop for themselves over a few years in language school. Perhaps, like the gift of tongues, the gift of teaching was there to give the ecclesias a running start. Over time more people would emerge with teaching skills, and teaching activity would become less dependent on the presence of Spirit-gifts.

But there is no question that teachers would always be crucial for the understanding and faith of the ecclesia: and one of Timothy's key responsibilities was to ensure a chain of faithful and competent men who could pass on Paul's gospel, undiminished, undistorted and undiluted, to a new generation of teachers, who should both teach their generation and pass on the content of the gospel to yet another generation of teachers, the precious "good deposit" of faith being handed from one generation to the next until Christ Jesus should re-appear (2 Timothy 2:1,2). Developing the next generation of teachers is still a critical responsibility if our community is to continue in "the truth of the gospel" until the Lord returns.

The importance of everyday teaching

Among the attributes Paul looked for in elder-overseers was skill in teaching (1 Timothy 3:2; Titus 1:9, cp. also 2 Timothy 2:24), and this remains an important attribute in those who lead us today. However, it would be a mistake to read Paul as requiring that ecclesial leaders must be competent to front a crowd and deliver a structured presentation. While structured, formal teaching has always been an important way of building understanding and stimulating faith in ecclesial life, since the first century, in fact, a view of teaching that sees only the platform is very blinkered.

Teaching encompasses a wide range of activities, as Paul told Timothy. His own instruction at the hands of his mother and grandmother took place beside his mattress, around the cooking pot, in the marketplace, on the way to and from the synagogue – something

Moses had drummed into Israel's parents in the beginning:

"You shall teach them diligently to your children, and shall talk of them when you sit in your house, and when you walk by the way, and when you lie down, and when thou rise."   (Deuteronomy 6:7)

Is this teaching any less important because it is informal and unstructured, stitched across the threads of everyday life? Surely it is the most important teaching work of all! According to Paul it was the substance of Timothy's understanding and faith, the thing to which he should look back when at any time he felt overwhelmed by the chaotic evil of the perilous times which would come, when people would not tolerate sound teaching, but would multiply teachers to suit their own tastes (2 Timothy 4:1-4). The instruction of Lois and Eunice would help Timothy to navigate the treacherous waters ahead, and it would also influence those who would be willing to listen to Timothy's teaching in turn.

Teaching in the kitchen and in the living room and in the bedroom, teaching in the car and in the shopping centre, is crucial if we are to pass the deposit of faith to the next generation. It is a work for father and mother, and by extension for brothers and sisters, and it is hard to see how any teaching work could be more important than this.

Did sisters teach?

Did sisters teach? Indeed they did. We have already considered the enormous contribution of Lois and Eunice. Sisters continue to play a crucial teaching role at home and at Sunday School. And the New Testament contains other important references.

Priscilla and Aquila, acting as a team, took Apollos aside and filled out his understanding of the Word of God, bridging the gap from the climactic prophetic ministry of John the Baptist to the glorious reality of Jesus Christ (Acts 18:26). Perhaps it was Priscilla who took the initiative in approaching Apollos, as in this place she is named first. On other occasions Aquila comes first. Those who knew only the baptism of John were re-baptized (19:1-6). So the instruction of Apollos was effectively the instruction of a candidate for baptism – in this case, a candidate well-versed in Scripture, but nevertheless one who had only limited knowledge of Jesus Christ. Here, therefore, is one very fruitful way in which sisters with a talent for teaching can apply their gifts.

The Bible Missions are always calling for competent teachers to answer the questions of their contacts and lead them toward faith and baptism. The fields are "white for harvest", but the challenge is, as it has always been, the shortage of labourers to bring in "the fulness of the Gentiles" (Matthew 9:36-38; Romans 11:25). Here is another opportunity for sisters who have teaching skills.

There is an important teaching work that is almost entirely the responsibility of sisters. Paul instructs Titus that "older women ... are to teach what is good, and so train the young women to love their husbands and children, to be self-controlled, pure, working at home, kind, and submissive to their husbands, that the word of God may not be reviled" (Titus 2:3,4).

Interestingly, Paul tells Titus, or implies, that he is to teach the older men, and the older women, and the younger men, and the slaves – but helping younger women to develop and apply godly life skills was not his brief. That was the work of older sisters, who would not simply download the wisdom they had learned from applying the Word of God to life's experiences, but would listen, encourage, counsel and mentor, and provide godly role models. There will always be a great need for sisters who are spiritually healthy and well grounded to provide help, sensitively, to other sisters around them who are in need of encouragement and advice.

So there are a number of important examples of sisters serving by teaching straight out of the New Testament; and for those with teaching gifts there are, therefore, many opportunities to use them.

18

AN APOSTOLIC PROHIBITION

BUT there is one important qualification that Paul places on teaching, and it goes hand in hand with a qualification on leadership. In his first letter to Timothy he makes the emphatic statement we have glanced at several times: "I do not permit a woman to teach or to exercise authority over a man" (1 Timothy 2:12).

Teaching and the exercise of authority

The first prohibition cannot be absolute. For one thing, Paul instructs Titus that older sisters should teach younger sisters. Here in 1 Timothy the setting is clearly the assembled ecclesia. Paul instructs the brothers to pray "in every place" (verse 8), and the sisters to present themselves in a way that is modest and does not draw attention to themselves (verse 9). He continues after this section by addressing the spiritual qualifications for elder-overseers and deacons (3:14,15), and concludes with a summary statement indicating that these are different aspects of how we ought to conduct ourselves in "the household of God, which is the church of the living God" (3:14,15). Paul's objection relates specifically to the teaching of the assembled ecclesia, not to teaching in general.

The second phrase sits alongside the first: "Nor to usurp authority over the man". The Greek verb *authenteo*, translated "to usurp authority" in the KJV, means "to exercise authority", and the KJV is rather too strong. It is sometimes suggested that the verb refers to the misuse of authority in a domineering, aggressive, harmful or even violent way. A comprehensive study reviewed eighty-five occurrences of the verb in ancient writings from the 1st century BC to the 10th century AD, and found no uses of it in a pejorative sense before the 4th century AD, more than 300 years after Paul wrote.* Other versions translate the verb "exercise authority" (ESV) or "have authority" (NIV).

It is clear what kind of authority Paul had in mind. In the very next chapter Paul discusses the spiritual qualifications for elder-overseers, who were ordained or appointed as shepherds to lead the flock of God, or, in another figure, stewards over his household. These elder-overseers were exclusively male, as the pronouns and the qualifications make clear: "the husband of one wife" (3:2,4).

Emphatic statements

"I suffer not", Paul says. This statement communicates to Timothy in his ecclesial context what is Paul's standard practice in all ecclesial contexts. As we shall see when we get to his first letter to the Corinthians, Paul was concerned that all brothers and sisters in all ecclesias should abide by apostolic teaching and practice in some core matters, while other issues, more to do with lifestyle, could be decided by local culture without affecting in any way their Christian commitment or witness. It is his practice not to 'give permission for' or tolerate teaching and the exercise of authority by sisters. He instructs Timothy to take the same approach.

Paul underlines the prohibition with a further strong statement. Sisters should not teach, or exercise authority, but be "in silence". This word can mean simply "silence", but it can also have a broader meaning. The indolent and the interfering are to work "quietly and to earn their own living" (2 Thessalonians

---

* H S Baldwin, "An Important Word: *Authenteo* in 1 Timothy 2:12", in A J Köstenberger and T R Schreiner (eds), *Women in the Church: An Analysis and Application of 1 Timothy 2:9-15* (2nd ed, Baker, 2005): pages 39-51. The book in which the study appears is an excellent academic treatment of this passage in its Biblical and cultural context.

3:12). It is not that they must work in silence, but that they must mind their own business, and cease to make trouble for other people. Similarly here: Paul does not insist that sisters should be absolutely silent, but that they should, as we might say, 'take a back seat,' allowing brothers to take the lead in teaching and governance.

Paul's first reason – from Creation

The force of Paul's statement is confronting, but he provides two reasons for his position, both taken from "the law": "For Adam was first formed, then Eve. And Adam was not deceived, but the woman being deceived was in the transgression."

What is especially powerful about Paul's reasoning is that he draws his first reason from God's arrangement before sin entered the world, and his second reason from the world as a result of human sin. The structure of his logic straddles the Fall: and that contradicts the idea that the different roles of man and woman in Christ are simply consequences of sin, that should now be set aside.*

The woman was created after the man, from the man, to help the man. Those facts are clearly stated in the second half of the Creation account, and that is Paul's first reason. Eve was to help Adam, not to supplant him. God's revelation was given to him, and he should pass it on to her, not she to him. Adam, not Eve, was to lead and teach.

---

* We note in passing that Paul makes no reference whatever to the Gnosticism or Diana-inspired feminism that some have proposed was infecting the ecclesia. Apart from the fact that Gnosticism was a second century, not a first century phenomenon, a review of the role of women in Ephesian society found that, while women played a positive role, it was not a feminist society, and there is no historical basis for "attempts to construe the present passage as Paul's effort to counteract unruly women in this city in Asia Minor" – S M Baugh, "A Foreign World: Ephesus in the First Century", in A J Köstenberger and T R Schreiner (eds), *Women in the Church*, pages 13-38.

We are clearly intended to understand that Adam and Eve are archetypes of man and woman in Christ: and as the logic of Paul's position is grounded in these Creation realities, they are not culturally bound, but as relevant in the twenty-first century as they were in the first; and in fact, in Eden itself.

Paul's words are a positive challenge to man and woman to fulfil the great destiny for which God has created us. The complementary roles of male and female, brother and sister, in the ecclesia spring from God's purpose in creating man and woman in the beginning. When a brother, therefore, teaches and exercises authority, he is fulfilling God's purpose for men from the beginning, and glorifies God. When a sister provides help and support, she is fulfilling God's purpose for women from the beginning, and glorifies God.

Paul's second reason – from the Fall

Paul's second reason is taken from the account of the Fall, when God's intent was disregarded. Eve opened her mind to the serpent, and his thinking supplanted the law of God in her mind. She was deceived: desire for what God had prohibited impelled her to sin. Adam was not deceived by the serpent, but joined her in sin nevertheless: and the catastrophe was complete. That is Paul's second reason: and again Adam and Eve are to be understood as archetypes of man and woman in Christ. Both were transgressors; and in fact the primary responsibility for sin entering the world is always laid on Adam, not on Eve.

Paul is not suggesting that the restrictions he has just spoken of are in any sense a punishment for sin. Rather, his words are a powerful warning to man and woman not to subvert God's purpose. When Eve took the initiative, and Adam went along with her action, God's intention that Adam should lead and Eve should help was ignored; and the consequences were devastating. Therefore, Paul insists, it is God's intention that brothers are to take the lead in teaching the assembled ecclesia, and exercising authority to ensure that the ecclesia outworks that teaching in its collective decisions and actions: and this despite the fact that, as other New Testament writings show, there are many sisters competent to teach.

"She will be saved"

To this warning Paul adds a strong assurance, "She will be saved", perhaps chiefly because he does not want any brother or sister to think that sisters are spiritually inferior, or less important to God. "She will be saved through childbearing – if they continue in faith and love and holiness, with self-control" (1 Timothy 2:15).

Paul knows full well that some sisters have never married, or having married have never borne children, but "childbearing" is representative of the many things that only women can do, and which faithful sisters will do exceptionally well.

The whole process of bringing up a family, starting with childbirth, and continuing in the nurture of children, young people, mature brothers and sisters who "continue in faith and love and holiness, with self-control" is one way – one way among many, but one very important way nevertheless – in which godly women can express the heartfelt faith in God that leads to salvation.

What greater challenge could there be for any person, male or female, than to embed in the next generation one's own deeply felt values of faith, love, holiness and moderation? Diligent teaching at home is a critical responsibility for fathers and mothers: and the same work of instilling Bible principles and knowledge and nurturing discipleship is extended in the teaching work of grandfathers and grandmothers, family friends and Sunday School teachers. Sisters often lead in this work: and there can be no teaching more important.

It was Jesus Christ who made Paul "an apostle … a teacher of the Gentiles in faith and truth" (2:7). To ignore what he actually does say in favour of what we might wish he had said, whatever our motive, is neither faithfulness to the Word of God, nor submission to the Lord Christ. This trend is evident in many Christian denominations about us; and it would be disappointing and disturbing if we were to see such thinking distracting us from "a sincere and pure devotion to Christ" (2 Corinthians 11:3) when we are on the verge of being presented to him by the apostle. Let us rather have the courage and faith to embrace God's purpose for His children, and receive the spiritual blessings that will follow richly for ourselves, our families and our community.

19

WORSHIPPING WITH THE HEAD
UNCOVERED AND COVERED

THERE is another matter relating to brothers and sisters in worship, and that is the display and the covering of the head, to which Paul dedicates half a chapter of his first letter to the Corinthians (11:1-16).

These verses sit in a larger context (chapters 11–14) dealing with ecclesial conduct. Many shared themes and common words tie this section together: the focus on the ecclesia (11:18,22, cp. 12:28; 14:4,5,12,19,23,28, 33-35), particularly at times when brothers and sisters "come together" (11:17,18,20,33,34, cp. 14:23,26) "in one place" (11:20, cp. 14:23); the contrast between behaviour "in the ecclesia" and "at home" (11:34, cp. 14:35); his warnings against "division" or "schism" (11:18, cp. 12:25), and his concern that the Corinthians care "one for another" (11:33, cp. 12:25). Finally, there is the particular interest in "women" (16 times in 11:2-15, cp. 14:34,35), and his caution against behaviour by man or woman that brings "shame" (11:6, cp. 14:35).

But Paul's two principal concerns are first, respect for the head, and second, care for the body. We must always begin with the Head: and that is what Paul does.

A maverick tendency corrected

It is not surprising that the issue of the head uncovered and covered crops up only the once. In most of his letters Paul needed to do little more than remind, or reinforce, or clarify. Most ecclesias did not challenge his authority, or his teaching, or the apostolic traditions that he had passed on to them. The Corinthians challenged all three. They had a strong maverick tendency; and a number of times Paul had to urge them, or command them, to come into line with accepted practice across the ecclesial world (1 Corinthians 4:17; 7:17; 11:34; 14:33b-37; 15:3,ff.; 16:1, with further hints in 1:2 and 10:32). Their autonomy was no defence when they were clearly out of line with apostolic teaching and ecclesial practice.

The apparent insistence on head covering by some brethren at Corinth, and the apparent rejection of head covering by some sisters, was also contrary to what he had taught them. Paul deliberately frames his discussion to make that point. He introduces it with a word of praise for the carefulness with which they were adhering to what he had taught them:

> "I commend you because you remember me in everything and maintain the traditions even as I delivered them to you." (11:1)

His commendation was not absolute, as the subsequent chapters show. They had corrupted the Lord's supper. They were grossly misusing the Spirit's gifts. They had turned the doctrine of the resurrection inside out. They had failed to follow through with collections for the poor Jewish brothers and sisters in Jerusalem. But Paul was always pleased to praise where he could. What is noteworthy is that he frames the matter of head coverings as a matter of scrupulously maintaining the traditions he had delivered to them. While we are right to keep human traditions firmly in their place, knowing the way in which they can easily corrupt or even replace the Word of God, the traditions of the apostles are good traditions, and it is part of our faithfulness to Christ, and what he first delivered to the apostles, to maintain those traditions they have delivered to us.*

---

* For more references on this theme, see further Acts 1:2; 10:48; 16:4; 1 Corinthians 7:10; 9:14; 11:23; 1 Thessalonians 4:2,11; 2 Thessalonians 2:15; 3:4,6,10,12; 1 Timothy 1:3; 4:11; 5:7; 6:13,17; Titus 1:5; 2:15; and 1 Corinthians 7:6,25; 2 Corinthians 8:8; Philemon 8.

No scope for argument

Paul concludes his discussion by reinforcing his opening hint with a blunt warning:

"If any man seem to be contentious, we have no such custom, neither the churches of God."

(11:16, KJV)

It has sometimes been suggested that Paul, having set out his view in some detail, and in very forceful language, is now finishing rather limply by conceding that the matter is not, after all, something to argue about. But this interpretation turns what Paul is saying on its head, as is evident from other leading translations:

"If anyone presumes to raise objections on this point – well, I acknowledge no other mode of worship." (Moffatt)

"If anyone is disposed to be contentious, we recognize no other practice." (RSV)

"If anyone wants to be contentious about this, we have no other practice." (NIV)

"If anyone is inclined to be contentious, we have no such practice." (ESV)

The "we" referred to is the other apostles (cp. 4:9-13; 9:1-6). Paul is saying, 'If anybody wishes to argue with what I have said, I want you to know that all of the apostles agree with what I have said, and so does every other ecclesia'. His opening words, "If anyone", perhaps imply that the innovation was being promoted by some in the ecclesia, rather than the ecclesia as a whole: as later with the new thinking on the resurrection, promoted by "some among you" (15:12). Corinth's tendency was not only maverick but fragmentary and schismatic, and it would be consistent with what we know about them for a minority group within the ecclesia to be ploughing its own furrow, despite the disruption it was creating.

In fact, the word translated "contentious" in the KJV refers not simply to somebody with an alternative point of view, but to that unfortunate character who comes to the fore from time to time, the "lover of quarrels". There were too many of these in Corinth, and as a consequence the ecclesia was riven with strife, which Paul had earlier identified as a sure sign that they were still spiritually undeveloped, or "carnal" (3:3).

The main point to note, however, is that Paul concludes the matter as he introduced it – in terms of their obligation to maintain the traditions of the apostles as practised in all other ecclesias.

All brothers and all sisters

Throughout this section Paul uses two Greek words we have already come across, with a broad and a narrow meaning, *aner* standing both for 'male' and 'husband' and *gune* for 'female' and 'wife'. Only the context can determine which sense is intended in each instance. The question naturally arises, Did Paul again have the marriage relationship in mind? Is he here referring to husbands and wives in worship, or more broadly to brothers and sisters? How are we to decide?

We can see immediately that some of his statements make no sense when applied to the husband-wife relationship. For example, "As the woman is of the man, even so is the man also by the woman" (11:12). The verse could not be translated, 'As the wife is of the husband, even so is the husband also by the wife'. Neither statement is true or sensible. Similarly with, 'The husband is not of the wife, but the wife of the husband' (verse 8). The first phrase is true, but the second is untrue.

Other statements read strangely when confined to husbands and wives. 'The head of every husband is Christ' (verse 3). 'A husband ... is the image and glory of God ... the wife is the glory of the husband' (verse 7). 'If a husband have long hair, it is a shame to him' (verse 16). Then what of other brothers? Were they free to cover their heads in worship, or let their hair grow long? Were unmarried women free to uncover their heads?

On the other hand, it is possible to translate the terms as "man" and "woman" consistently through the passage, as does the King James Version. Many translations oscillate between the broad and the narrow meaning within the one passage, which is inherently unlikely. Paul's words are comprehensive – "every man" (verses 3,4), "every woman" (verse 5) – and he intended them to cover all brothers and all sisters.

An ecclesial context

There are also good reasons for concluding that Paul's discussion relates to public ecclesial worship, not private relationships. It is followed by two sections that deal with ecclesial meetings (11:17-34; chapters 12–14). The words that introduce Paul's discussion of the memorial meeting – "Now in this that I declare unto you I praise you not" (11:17) – directly reference and contrast with the words that introduce his discussion of the head symbolism – "Now I commend you ..." (11:2). (The same Greek verb is translated "commend" in the first instance and "praise" in the second.) Paul highlights the fact that his instruction is in line with "custom" in all "the churches of God" (11:16). His specific mention of praying and prophesying also indicates that he has a group setting in mind (11:4,5,13): for prophecy was a gift intended for the benefit of others (14:4), and the praying here referred to is probably also the Spirit-gifted prayer to which he later refers (14:14-16).

Finally, the practices on which Paul is commenting suggest that he is speaking of conduct in the assembled ecclesia rather than at home. At home neither men nor women would have felt any impulse to cover their heads in private worship. The question only arose with respect to their conduct in public, among other men and women. There is a significant difference between the private world of the family home, in which lavish meals or free-flowing discussion might be appropriate, and the public setting of the ecclesial assembly, in which restraint is required – as Paul points out (11:22,34;

14:35). The fact that meetings were often held in large private houses does not alter the fact that what is appropriate in the one public setting is often not appropriate in the other private setting.

Is this passage an extended quotation from the Judaists?

It is sometimes suggested that the passage has been drastically misunderstood. This is one of those occasions on which Paul quotes the Corinthians in order to set them straight, it is argued. Paul is not insisting that brothers should uncover their heads, and sisters cover them. Rather, these positions were novel ideas originating from Corinth, and he is arguing against them.

It is true that in this letter Paul does occasionally quote current sayings in the ecclesia at Corinth with which he disagrees. Examples that are generally accepted as quotations of this kind include:

"All things are lawful for me ..."
(twice in 1 Corinthians 6:12)

"Food is meant for the stomach and the stomach for food" (verse 13)

"It is good for a man not to have sexual relations with a woman" (7:1)

"All of us possess knowledge" (8:1)

These quotations are generally Corinthian justifications of licence, self-indulgence and self-will, although the third statement springs from an ascetic point of view. All of them are short and pithy one-line epigrams, which Paul immediately qualifies or contradicts sharply and unambiguously, so that the reader is in no doubt of where he stands. In other places Paul plainly indicates that he is quoting: for example, "How can some of you say ..." (15:12).

These features are not present in 1 Corinthians 11:2-16. The words of verse 3 are indisputably Paul's, and the words of verses 4 and 5 flow from verse 3 without any kind of indication that they contain a quotation from another source. There is no evidence to indicate that at any point Paul is quoting from the Corinthians, and this novel suggestion has to be rejected as an unjustifiable and improper attempt to prevent Paul speaking for himself.

Why did these issues arise?

Why did these issues arise at all? At some point Jewish men began to cover their heads in synagogue worship, although it is not certain whether this practice was established in the first century. Greeks typically worshipped bareheaded, but Roman men sometimes drew the folds of their mantle or toga over their heads in worship. Men who had worshipped with the head covered for cultural reasons might well think it appropriate to carry over their established worship practices into the ecclesia. In other ecclesias nobody had challenged what the apostles had laid down as Christian practice, but in Corinth, with its maverick tendency, there were those who felt free to ignore apostolic teaching.

Respectable women, on the other hand, covered their heads in public, whether Roman, Greek, Syrian or Jewish, and high-class Jewish women even veiled their faces entirely, in the manner common among devout Muslims today.* Clearly some sisters in Corinth were uncovering their heads in ecclesial worship.

Paul does not involve himself in any discussion about their motivations. He deals directly with their practice. But can we imagine what might have motivated this challenge to his teaching? Perhaps they reasoned that they had been created in God's image and likeness (Genesis 1:26,27): they were "one in Christ Jesus" (Galatians 3:28): they had gifts of the Spirit just like their brothers in Christ: well, they would assert their equality and claim their place among the Spirit-gifted brothers, even though it meant ignoring Paul's teaching. In uncovering his head the man declared his

---

* J Jeremias, *Jerusalem in the Time of Jesus*, pages 359-361.

intention to submit to the will of God, His ultimate head. In uncovering her head, the woman declared her independence from the man.

W F Barling thinks there was something more:

"What in reality motivated them was not Christian self-respect, but a spirit of jealousy and rivalry – doubtless admixed, in the case of any sisters with particularly beautiful hair, with a strong element of vanity also. The result was an exhibitionism which was the negation of all that was truly feminine."*

Some combination of these motives was no doubt what lay behind the thinking of those sisters at Corinth who had begun to uncover their heads in worship.

---

* W F Barling, *The Letters to Corinth*, page 119.

20

THE GLORY OF GOD AND
THE GLORY OF MAN

"The head of every man is Christ"

ET us turn to what Paul says, then, and work our
way through it systematically. It is characteristic
of his approach that he first lays down a doctrinal
principle as the basis for a discipleship practice: "The
head of every man is Christ" (1 Corinthians 11:3).

The resurrection of Jesus Christ was the first step in
a process by which God elevated his Son to be "the head
over all things", "far above all rule and authority and
power and dominion, and above every name that is
named, not only in this age but also in the one to come"
(Ephesians 1:20,21, cp. Colossians 1:18). But God "gave
him as head over all things to the church, which is his
body, the fullness of him who fills all in all" (Ephesians
1:22,23, cp. Colossians 2:9,10). His authority is
comprehensive, but his relationship with the ecclesia is
special. God has given the head to the body. The body is
the full expression of all that the head is. And yet it is
the head "who fills all in all".*

The notion that the Greek word *kephale*, "head", is
used in the sense of "source", has become very
widespread in discussions about the roles of men and
women since it was first proposed by Stephen Bedale in
1954. However, an examination of over 2,000 instances
has shown conclusively that the meaning "source" is not
attested in Greek literature before the ninth century
AD, and does not occur in the Septuagint, which Paul
quotes frequently; while the meaning "leader or
authority" is common. The meaning "source" is not
given in the leading reference for New Testament

---

* For a comprehensive discussion see W Grudem, *Evangelical
Feminism and Biblical Truth*, pages 200, 201, 544-599.

Greek, Bauer-Danker-Andt-Gingrich's *Greek-English Lexicon of the New Testament and Other Early Christian Literature* (3rd edition, 2001), and other relevant lexicons agree.

When Scripture speaks of Christ as the head it is either with respect to his preeminence as "the head of the corner" (Matthew 21:42; Mark 12:10; Luke 20:17; Acts 4:11; 1 Peter 2:7); his authority as "the head of every man" (1 Corinthians 11:3), "the head over all things" (Ephesians 1:22; Colossians 1:18) or "the head of all rule and authority" (Colossians 2:10); or his relationship to the ecclesia, over which he is set, and which he inspires, nourishes and coordinates (Ephesians 1:22; 4:15; 5:23; Colossians 1:18; 2:10,19). In the context of Scripture, that is what the metaphor of the "head" means.

In the fourth chapter Paul expands the metaphor. The body, "speaking the truth in love", grows up into the head: from the head the whole body is inspired and coordinated and energised to ensure that all members grow together, and toward the head, in love (Ephesians 4:11-16, cp. Colossians 2:19). In the fifth chapter he extends the relationship between Christ and ecclesia to husband and wife. He calls on the wife to show to her husband the submission and respect the ecclesia shows toward Christ. He calls on the husband to show to his wife the commitment and love and self-sacrifice and spiritual nurture that Christ showed, and shows, toward his ecclesia (Ephesians 5:22-33). The doctrinal metaphor of Christ's headship is stated, expanded and extended to human relationships. And in his first letter to the Corinthians Paul likewise extends the metaphor to human relationships, in the very next phrase: "The head of the woman is the man."

Headship is not only about the relationship between man and woman, or between man and Christ. Christ himself has a head: "The head of Christ is God." What God asks of man and woman, therefore, is the extension of what He has already asked, and received, from His

Son: an acceptance of His arrangements, the affirmation, "Thy will be done", and the submission that accompanies that affirmation. And not only in the past and the present: for the grand finale of the new millennium will be the transfer of the kingdom from the Son to the Father:

> "Then the Son himself will also be subjected to him who put all things in subjection under him, that God may be all in all." (1 Corinthians 15:27,28)

What Christ yielded to the Father with all his heart is surely good enough for us, whether male or female.

Honour and dishonour

How, then, are we to express our acceptance of God's arrangements? Curiously, this section is generally considered to be about the covering of the head by sisters. In fact, Paul first comments on the way brothers present themselves for worship. The section is about two complementary aspects of one practice, and Paul's discussion of these aspects is intertwined.

"Every man who prays or prophesies with his head covered dishonours his head" (11:4). The proximate head is Christ, and the ultimate head is God. Man honours Christ, and therefore God, by worshipping with his head uncovered. Man dishonours or shames Christ, and therefore God, by worshipping with his head covered – a powerful statement that must concern any Christian eager to honour his God.

Paul does not yet supply a reason for this statement, but turns instead to woman. He comments on the way sisters present themselves for worship: "Every woman who prays or prophesies with her head uncovered dishonours her head" (11:5, NKJV). For sisters, his position is reversed: to uncover their heads is dishonourable. The woman's proximate head is the man, whose head is Christ, whose head is God. Woman dishonours man, and therefore Christ, and therefore God, by worshipping with her head uncovered.

114

Again Paul does not immediately supply a reason for this statement; but he does add, rather forcefully, "since it is the same as if her head were shaven" (11:5b,6). This is a plain reference to the way in which immoral women were shamed by cutting off their hair. Interestingly, the only time the Law required a woman to present herself bare-headed before God was when her husband suspected her of adultery, and brought her before the priest for trial (Numbers 5:18). 'A godly woman would never present herself in that way', Paul argues: 'then let her cover her head during worship.'

The image and glory of God

Now Paul sets out the principle on which his instruction is founded:

"For a man ought not to cover his head, since he is the image and glory of God."   (11:7)

Paul is citing the Creator: "Let us make man in our image, after our likeness" (Genesis 1:26,27), as interpreted by David: "You … have crowned him with glory and honour" (Psalm 8:5).

Paul's reference is not to Adam, but to Christ, "his head". It is Christ who is "the image and glory of God" (2 Corinthians 4:4; Colossians 1:15). Man is born "in Adam", and, like Seth, is created "in his own likeness, after his image" (Genesis 5:1,3), which Paul styles "the image of the earthy" (1 Corinthians 15:49). In Christ, however, he is recreated "the new man", "conformed to the image of His Son" (Romans 8:29; 2 Corinthians 3:18), which after God is created "in righteousness and true holiness" (Ephesians 4:23,24; Colossians 3:10), and is, like Christ, "full of grace and truth" (John 1:14).

The "image and glory" referred to by Paul is not the old man's natural likeness to Adam, who subsequently fell from God's "image and glory", but the new man's spiritual likeness to Christ, "his head", into which all believers, male and female, are changed day by day. As the man honours this likeness, he honours God's

115

purpose in creating him, honours His purpose in newly recreating him in Christ, and glorifies his Maker.

The glory of the man

It is important that we remind ourselves that this is also true of the woman. But there is a difference. From Genesis 1, Paul moves to Genesis 2. He continues, "The woman is the glory of the man" (11:7). Equal under God – as Genesis 1 shows – male and female nevertheless were created for different roles – as Genesis 2 shows. The statement is somewhat confronting, but Paul immediately explains what he means: "For man was not made from woman, but woman from man. Neither was man created for woman; but woman for man" (11:8,9).

The way in which Paul draws on Genesis 2 is consistent with his exposition in 1 Timothy 2, and we remind ourselves of the three Creation principles that are fundamental to his thinking. Woman is "after the man", for Adam was created first; she is "of the man", created from Adam's side; and she is "for the man", created to be his helper (11:8,9).

These are Creation principles, not outcomes of the Fall or cultural artefacts, and Paul's teaching is based firmly on them. The woman glorifies her Maker by fulfilling God's special purpose in creating her after the man, from the man, to complement and help the man. For this reason Paul can describe her as "the glory of the man", even as she glorifies God.

As we gather for worship

We must remember that in this section Paul is focusing on the way in which brothers and sisters present themselves for worship. It was appropriate that the Jewish man, living under the Law, should cover his head, effectively recognising that "all have sinned, and fall short of the glory of God" (Romans 3:23). But the glory of God was also proclaimed: for as the priests served in the Tabernacle, their bodies covered by white linen from the top of their head to the toes of their feet in the presence of God (Exodus 29:4-9), the high priest bore bravely on his forehead a golden plate inscribed, "Holiness to the Lord" (28:36-38). The glory of man submitted to the glory of God, the sinfulness of man was covered by the righteousness provided by God, the people and their offerings were hallowed, and God accepted His people, and reconciled them to Himself.

In Christ, as Paul teaches, the man should appear before God bareheaded, symbolically projecting the glory of God in worship. The woman for her part should appear before God with her head covered, symbolically obscuring the glory of man in worship, in keeping with the principle "that no human being might boast in the presence of God" (1 Corinthians 1:29). When brothers and sisters present themselves for worship in this way, the head and the body, Christ and all his fulness, are symbolically projected in worship to the Father. The glory of man is veiled, and the glory of God manifested, complementary statements that all believers, male and female, endorse.

Why should it be the brothers who manifest the glory of God in this mute symbol? God consistently represents Himself to us as male throughout Scripture – as a Father, for example, and as a King. He is spoken of as male, without exception.* While some have speculated that angels, "the sons of God", may be both male and female, where Scripture mentions their apparent gender it is always male. Brothers, therefore, take this role. Appropriately, sisters take the role of the ecclesia, the Bride of Christ, veiling the glory of man before the glory of God. A beautiful spiritual drama is played out for those with eyes to see as the two sexes cooperate in glorifying God.

Authority on her head, because of the angels

Others, unobserved, are present as the ecclesia assembles for worship. The angels who rejoiced in the unfolding spectacle of the first creation take a keen

---

* We are indebted to John Morris for drawing our attention to this important point.

interest in God's plan (1 Peter 1:12), and are present to witness the development of the new creation and help it forward (cp. also 4:9; 1 Timothy 5:21; Hebrews 1:14) – the same angels with whom Eve and Adam, contrary to God's purpose, had sought equality, a self-assertion which was itself sin, and which every believer rejects. Brothers and sisters alike should remember these silent watchers and ministers, and honour God's purpose in creation, the one by symbolically uncovering the head, the other by symbolically covering the head.

This covering is what Paul means by "power on her head" (11:10, KJV), paraphrased by other translations as "a sign of authority" (RV) or "a symbol of authority" (ESV). Verses 8,9 are a parenthetical justification of Paul's statement that "the woman is the glory of the man" (verse 7), and this comment also goes back to that statement.* Because she is, in Paul's words, "the glory of the man", she "ought", that is, "she has an obligation" to bear upon her head a sign of her submission to God's arrangements, and ultimately to God as Head over all. Yet Paul may be saying something more than this. She has the authority, he writes. It lies with her. While she is under an obligation, that obligation is not thrust upon her. Paul asks of her a voluntary acceptance of God's arrangements. As in Christ we are free to serve, so she has authority to submit.

An important balance

Paul is quick, however, to add an important balancing comment – the balance that is in the Bible's treatment of this subject from the earliest chapters of Genesis.

Brothers and sisters should never fall into the trap of thinking each other somehow unnecessary or redundant, more or less important to God. "Nevertheless", he cautions, "in the Lord woman is not independent of man nor man of woman; for as woman was made from man, so man is now born of woman" (11:11,12). Even in the natural order, while Eve might

---

* Although the NIV neatly captures the logic of the verse: "For this reason [i.e., verse 8], and because of the angels ..."

have been made from Adam, every man since that time has owed his existence and upbringing to the pain and sacrificial love of his mother.

"And all things are from God", Paul concludes, anxious as always to keep things in perspective for the Corinthians by reminding them of their utter dependence on Him.

"Spiritual wholeness is not attainable in any community – let alone the Christian – unless each element, the male and the female alike, makes its own distinctive contribution to that community's life."*

An appeal to their own spiritual judgment

To his Scriptural reasoning Paul adds a final appeal to their own sense of what was appropriate. "Judge among yourselves. Is it proper for a woman to pray to God with her head uncovered?" (11:13, NKJV). "Is it fitting that at such a time she should assert herself, attract attention, and project the glory of man?" The rhetorical question points directly to a negative answer. It is inappropriate.

Paul puts a second question. "Does not nature itself teach you that if a man wears long hair it is a disgrace for him?" (11:14). A man with long hair has blurred the distinctiveness of male and female. His maleness is obscured, and his effeminate presentation is "a disgrace for him", as our God-given instincts should tell us.

For a woman the reverse is true. Longer hair, covering her head, is her glory, "For her hair is given to her for a covering" (11:15). This has confused some, who have asked whether Paul, having insisted on a sister covering her head in worship, is now proposing that her hair is that covering, or alternatively that her hair is given her instead of a veil or scarf. But two quite different Greek words are used. When Paul insists that a sister cover her head, the Greek verb *katakalupto* is used, meaning "to cover the head". Here the Greek noun *peribolaion* is used, a general word referring to a piece of clothing such as a wrap, cloak, robe or mantle

---

* W F Barling, *The Letters to Corinth*, p 120.

(cp. Hebrews 1:12). A woman's hair is integral to the way she presents herself to the world. It is a recognised aspect of her natural beauty, a gift from God, although like any gift it may be misused – Peter and Paul had to caution against the ostentatious display of elaborate, expensive or fashionable hairstyles (1 Timothy 2:9; 1 Peter 3:3,4).

The true nature of man and woman as God created them is not to be obscured or distorted, but to shine through, and specially as we bow before God in worship, and submit ourselves to the headship of the Lord Christ.

Important symbolic acts

Is every man, therefore, the head of every woman? Does every brother have authority over every sister in every department of her life? Of course not. Paul never saw the relation between brother and sister in that way. He instructs the man in one thing only – that he should uncover his head. And he instructs the woman in one thing only – that she should cover her head. There is nothing more. The actions are symbolic, for male and female the outward expression of an inward orientation to the will of God, and an acceptance from the heart of His arrangements.

Are these actions therefore trivial, or optional? Then we may discard baptism and the Lord's supper. After all, they are only symbolic – are they not? Who would think that dunking a believer in a pool of water would be the solemn expression of their union with Christ, their faith in the resurrection from the dead, and their commitment to a new life of righteousness and service? Who would think that nibbling on a piece of bread and sipping from a glass of wine would be the focus of our devotion in remembering the love and sacrifice of the Lord Jesus? Yet "the foolishness of God is wiser than men" (1:25). These simple things, which are folly in the eyes of many, and a stumbling block to faith, God has invested with profound spiritual significance: and it is hard to imagine that any disciple would even consider throwing over those apostolic ordinances. They are symbolic: but then God has always taught through symbols, in the Old Testament and the New. We rightly honour these important symbolic acts.

It is peculiar that while so many brothers and sisters put so much store by the second half of the eleventh chapter of Paul's letter to the Corinthians, some put so little store by the first half. As Paul saw it, both matters were important aspects of an ecclesial order that was acceptable to God, and he therefore writes forcefully on both. Other things could wait until he came to Corinth (11:34), but these deviations from apostolic teaching and practice had to be set right as soon as possible.

So stands Paul's teaching: and those who acknowledge his authority today, as "an apostle of Jesus Christ", will be quick to accept his reasoning and honour it in their practice.

21

SILENCE IN THE ECCLESIA

THERE is one more passage that bears specifically on the place of man and woman in the ecclesia. Paul writes:

"The women should keep silent in the churches. For they are not permitted to speak, but should be in submission, as the Law also says. If there is anything they desire to learn, let them ask their husbands at home. For it is shameful for a woman to speak in church." (1 Corinthians 14:34,35)

Here the words "keep silent" really do mean "silence". But what does Paul mean by "speak"? The Greek *laleo* is used an extraordinary 24 times in chapter 14. On each prior occasion, and again in verse 39, it refers to inspired speech. It would be a remarkable thing if Paul suddenly switched meanings after such consistency. We conclude that here also Paul refers to inspired speech, and that he is therefore prohibiting the use of tongues and prophecy by sisters in the ecclesia.

It is important to note here that sisters are not the only group required to be silent in the context of Paul's teaching about appropriate use of the Spirit-gifts. Those with the gift of tongues are required to be silent if no interpreter is present (verse 28). Even the authoritative prophets are to pause if God gives a new revelation during the course of an ecclesial meeting (verse 30).

Paul considered these commandments to be consistent with his teaching that "God is not a God of confusion but of peace" (verse 33). The silence he requires of sisters "in the ecclesias" flows from these other constraints. He chastised the Corinthians for taking an independent stance (verse 36), and demanded that they acknowledge his teaching as "a command of the Lord" (verse 37).

Some alternative suggestions

It is sometimes suggested that Paul is laying down instruction which is specific to the situation at Corinth: but his use of the plural "churches" and his reference to "all churches of the saints" in the previous verse (verse 33) indicate that, like his earlier teaching on head coverings (11:16), he is enjoining a practice which is the accepted apostolic standard across the ecclesial world.

It is also sometimes suggested that the verses are actually a quotation by Paul of a position put to him by the Corinthians, with which he is thought to disagree.* But the words that follow make it clear that Paul is affirming the teaching in these two verses as "a commandment of the Lord", and he calls upon the Corinthians to affirm it also.

It has even been suggested that the verses are a later addition to the letter. This is the most extraordinary suggestion of all, for every manuscript contains them, every modern translation includes them, and almost all textual critics consider them original. A handful of manuscripts transpose the verses. These are chiefly "Western" manuscripts, well known to textual critics for their rather cavalier approach to the text of Scripture. Even so, there is no hint that any scribe considered the verses inauthentic. We can safely conclude that they are original, and that the one or two scholars who argue against their authenticity do so because they find the verses inconvenient.

Silence in ecclesial meetings

Nevertheless, even when we accept the authority of Paul's teaching, it poses some challenges. Was the silence to be absolute? How can it be reconciled with his earlier recognition of sisters praying or prophesying,

---

* A similar argument is put with respect to 1 Corinthians 11:2-16, and the reader is referred to the discussion in chapter 19.

apparently in ecclesial meetings? And what is the basis for his allusion to the law?

First, Paul's instruction relates specifically to ecclesial meetings. This is clear from the context. Paul refers to the times when the ecclesia "comes together" (11:17,33; 14:26) "in one place" (11:20; 14:23), or "in the ecclesia" (11:18; 12:28; 14:19,28), and contrasts their practice at such times with what they might do in their own houses (11:22,34). Some things that are appropriate at home are not appropriate in the assembled ecclesia.

This distinction is even more obvious when we consider that many ecclesial meetings would have been held in large private homes owned by wealthy believers. They could eat and drink to their heart's content – but not when their house was full to overflowing with their brethren and sisters, many of whom were poor, or even slaves. When they came together in formal ecclesial meetings they were "the ecclesia of God". They must consider, honour and care for each other. In such a setting, Paul ruled, sisters were not to speak: at home, however, they were encouraged to "ask their husbands".

Not an absolute silence

Was the silence to be absolute? Paul does not proscribe praise and worship. Neither should we think that Paul is referring to every occasion on which more than one or two brothers and sisters come together. He refers to the memorial meetings of the ecclesia. Perhaps for most ecclesias that was the only meeting of the week. Today we tend to have a much greater variety of meetings. Ecclesial business meetings, or reading groups, or discussion groups are not the kind of meeting that Paul describes in chapters 11–14. Formal ecclesial meetings for prophecy and teaching, prayer and praise are what he has in mind, and especially the memorial meeting.

We should be looking to honour the spirit of Paul's teaching and practice, neither transforming it into a blanket of absolute silence, nor tossing it off completely as outdated or irrelevant. In the absence of further specific instruction from Paul, we must be guided by his principles.

If we seek a balance, then at our formal, structured meetings, such as the Memorial Meeting, our sisters should observe Paul's constraint; whereas at less formal, less structured meetings, such as business meetings, reading or discussion groups and short meetings at social get-togethers, our sisters might contribute without in any way challenging Paul's principles.

But every ecclesia must decide for itself, and every member must decide for himself or herself: and if the principles are honoured, even if in slightly different ways, then ecclesias may live in mutual respect and acceptance, as the Lord Jesus Christ would wish.

Paul's Scriptural reasoning

What is the basis for Paul's allusion to the law? The statement is not specific, and the difficulty is compounded by the fact that Paul uses the term "the law" in different ways in different contexts. Several alternatives have been proposed:

(1) The reference is to Genesis 3:16, "Your desire shall be for your husband, and he shall rule over you". As we have already indicated, however, we believe that these words were not God's intention for their relationship after the Fall, but His indication of what would be the inevitable but undesirable and sinful consequences of the Fall.

(2) The reference is to the law of vows (Numbers 30), or to the provisions of the Law more generally. This is possible, and may be subsumed under the third point.

(3) The reference is generally to the consistent pattern of teaching throughout the Old Testament: and in fact Paul's term "the law" includes the prophet Isaiah in the immediate context (verse 21). The fact that Paul does not go

on to cite a specific Scripture suggests that this is the most likely interpretation.

While it is not possible to be absolutely certain about the allusion, it is important to note both that Paul is very certain of his authority to lay down this ruling, and that he considered "the law", the teaching of Scripture specifically or generally, to be in perfect harmony with his commandment.

An avid desire to know the will of God was to be encouraged, but not in a way which cut across God's principles. Instead, it should become an opportunity for husband and wife to deepen their relationship around the things of God at home. This was not possible for Corinth's single sisters, of course: but then Paul is not trying to cover every conceivable angle. The important point is that "all things should be done decently and in order" (verse 40), the role of sisters in formal meetings of the ecclesia being one of those things.

Can 1 Corinthians 14 be reconciled with 1 Corinthians 11?

One final, important question remains. How can Paul's teaching in these verses be reconciled with his earlier recognition of sisters praying or prophesying, apparently in ecclesial meetings? Again, different explanations have been proposed:

(1) We are meant to understand that praying and prophesying by women possessing miraculous Spirit gifts (1 Corinthians 11) were exceptions to the rule about silence (1 Corinthians 14). This is possible, but unlikely, as Paul does not highlight them as exceptions in 1 Corinthians 14, even when he deals at length with the practice of tongues and prophecy.

(2) Paul is requiring silence only with respect to the judging of prophecies (verse 29), because this would put sisters in authority over brothers. Questions could easily be used to challenge the validity of a prophecy, even where direct

contradiction was avoided, and hence Paul proscribed questions also. Apart from this issue, sisters are not required to be silent at ecclesial meetings. Again, this option is possible: but it does not sit well with the flow of thought, and it is not easy to see the Corinthians themselves understanding Paul's words in this way.

(3) Paul's primary concern in chapter 11 was to establish the proper relationship between God and Christ, male and female in the ecclesia, and to require head coverings at ecclesial meetings as an expression of that relationship. He did not deal with the fact that sisters were speaking, even though he did in fact object to it, because that was a side issue: the big issue was the head. The prohibition on speaking comes later, when he is dealing with the proper conduct of ecclesial meetings (1 Corinthians 14). The apparent contradiction is simply a product of the fact that Paul deals with the issues in context, one at a time. Inspired speech was a valuable gift given to sisters as well as to brothers, but it was to be used at appropriate times and places, in private, in the home rather than in public, in the ecclesia.

We find the last option the most convincing in the context. It also agrees with Paul's instruction in 1 Timothy 2 about teaching and the exercise of authority, which would certainly have included prophecy, a directive word from God.

22

YOU ARE ALL ONE IN CHRIST JESUS

PERHAPS Paul's teaching is culturally bound, important in its day and age, but no longer relevant in the twenty-first century. The principles should be observed, but the specific practices can be set aside as culturally relative. The question is important, for it cuts to the heart of the whole issue. Should we continue to follow the practice of the apostles? Or should we adjust their first-century words and ways to conform with twenty-first century thinking about appropriate roles for men and women in the ecclesia of God?

Culturally bound?

We feel bound to point out that Paul was not constrained by tradition or convention, any more than the Lord Jesus was. He was quite prepared to take on the Sabbath, circumcision, the food taboos, the Law itself and the Jewish establishment. He was equally prepared to tell the Gentiles that many socially accepted practices – for example, idolatry, sexual promiscuity and homosexual practices – were not acceptable in Christ.

Furthermore, cultural practices differed widely even in Paul's day. As we have said, Jewish and Roman men, but not Greek men, might worship with the head covered. Paul countered this – it was inappropriate, even "dishonourable", whatever might be culturally acceptable.

Paul never bases his arguments on tradition or convention, but on timeless foundation principles that are not culturally relative – the relationship between man, woman, Christ and God; God's purpose in creating mankind, and His special purpose in creating woman when and as He did; the work of the angels in the natural and spiritual creation.

"The preaching of the cross" (1 Corinthians 1:18,23; 2:2) was fundamentally counter-cultural in Paul's day, challenging Jewish and Gentile ideas of what was right and proper, setting the foolishness and weakness of God against the wisdom and power of the world. It continues to be counter-cultural today. We must not, therefore, bend the teaching and practice of the apostles out of shape to accommodate society's expectations. The gospel, and the ecclesia, should continue to challenge our society, Western or Eastern, first world or third world. The apostles were Jesus' men. Despite what presently appears, the new millennium belongs to them, and those who, with them, follow his steps.

"You are all one in Christ Jesus"

What does Paul mean, then, by his statements of our unity in Christ? He writes:

"There is neither Jew nor Greek, there is neither slave nor free, there is no male nor female, for you are all one in Christ Jesus." (Galatians 3:28)

And again:

"For in one Spirit we were all baptized into one body – Jews or Greeks, slaves or free – and all were made to drink of one Spirit. For the body does not consist of one member but of many."
(1 Corinthians 12:13,14)

And again:

"Put on the new self, which is being renewed in knowledge after the image of its creator. Here there is not Greek and Jew, circumcised and uncircumcised, barbarian, Scythian, slave, free; but Christ is all, and in all." (Colossians 3:10,11)

Paul does not mean that the fundamental biology which determines our sex, or the historical factors which have defined our ethnicity or place in the family, or the social circumstances into which we have been born or placed

129

– that these things have simply disappeared: for in the verses that follow in Colossians, for example, as in Ephesians 5–6 and Titus 2, he spells out the differing application of the Christ-likeness in wives and husbands, children and fathers, slaves and masters – as does Peter in his first letter. A wife is still a wife, a husband is still a husband, a slave is still a slave, and a master is still a master.

Yet there is no contradiction between these facts, and Paul's magnificently true statements about our destiny in Christ, and the apostolic traditions he lays down for ecclesial life. Nationality, class, gender, age, era, location, descent – such things do not simply disappear, but they have no bearing on our value to God, our capacity to be recreated in His image and likeness, our redemption and our salvation, our destiny to enter the Kingdom of the Father, to serve with Christ and to reign with Christ.

It is beyond challenge that in these passages Paul is reaffirming one of the most central truths of our salvation: that regardless of who we are or where we have come from, if we believe in the living God, His promises are ours to inherit in Christ, who is everything to us, and whose likeness begins to develop in each of us from the moment of faith, a spiritual embryo nurtured by the living God through His living Word, until at last we are His full-grown sons and daughters, charged with His glory. That is the true gospel, and that is the faith, hope, love and joy of those who believe that gospel.

It is this shared experience of believing in God and receiving His grace; of being baptized into His Son and being integrated into one body; of bring recreated by God, filled by Christ, focused on Christ – it is this that makes us one in Christ.

The passage does not speak about relations between brothers and sisters, or their roles in governance and service. In fact, Galatians as a whole does not touch on these matters – at all. To read the passage as if it dealt with these questions is to misappropriate a great truth.

23

FIRST CENTURY TEACHING IN
THE TWENTY-FIRST CENTURY ECCLESIA

WHEN we began this study we set out to understand the will of God for the man and the woman He made in His image, and to do that we have criss-crossed the Scriptures. It may be helpful, as we conclude, to step back and see what we have learned.

Before we opened the Bible, we noted that society had experienced great changes in the roles and relationships of men and women over the last 150 years, but we resolved to let the Scriptures be our guide. The gospel is not hostile, for it springs from God's love for men and women: but it is, and always has been, fundamentally and radically counter-cultural, challenging the presuppositions and theses and conclusions which pass for wisdom in the world, setting over against them the cross of Christ, the foolishness and weakness of God, wiser and more powerful than anything of human origin. Our commitment as Christ's people is to proclaim the gospel to the world, to shine the light into the darkness, and to 'walk as children of light'.

This is especially important now that the 'last days' are upon us: for we are warned by Christ and his apostles that these will be particularly difficult times. We need to be vigilant, we are told; to be faithful to apostolic teaching, diligent with apostolic practice, patient with those who deviate from both.

Our understanding and practice with respect to the roles of brothers and sisters in the home and in the ecclesia is no exception. A world that cares nothing for the Lord Jesus or his apostles, refuses their authority, and rejects their teaching is a challenging context for faithful discipleship and a spiritually sound ecclesial life. So what is the twenty-first century ecclesia to do with first century teaching and practice?

Authority

With respect to leadership, it is clear that it was Paul's practice to prohibit the exercise of authority by sisters in ecclesias (1 Timothy 2:5-18), and by that he meant the work of elder-overseers, who were to shepherd the ecclesia, to be the Lord's stewards over his household (3:1-7). The nearest modern equivalent is our ecclesial Arranging Committee. It would be inappropriate for sisters to serve on that Committee.

At the same time, we recognise that sisters do not lack the skills or the spiritual qualifications to contribute at this level. We should heed the wise counsel of Brother Roberts, cited in the first chapter, and actively seek the observations and suggestions of our sisters. Their input was highly valued in the first century; and should be valued just as highly in the twenty-first century. We should be very foolish not to seek input from our sisters at every opportunity.

But there are many other opportunities to serve. We suggest that committees that serve the whole ecclesia – typically for preaching, for welfare, for youth activities, or for special events – should be chaired by a brother, although they should generally include any and all brothers and sisters with relevant gifts. This would seem to be an appropriate way to recognise in our times the principle underlying the apostles' decision to appoint seven brothers "over the business" of welfare, while no doubt involving many others in that work.

Prophecy and teaching

The Spirit-gifts of prophecy, teaching and praying are not active at present. Even if they were, we should be bound to respect Paul's requirements that women not teach men, and that women should keep silence "in the ecclesia" (1 Corinthians 14:34,35). As we have seen, however, the requirement for silence is not absolute,

133

and in less formal, less structured gatherings such as business meetings, reading or discussion groups and short meetings at social get-togethers, our sisters might contribute without in any way challenging Paul's principles.

Other opportunities for service

Aside from these significant restrictions, however, there are many areas in which sisters can use their gifts. Deacons were both men and women, although men predominated. There were many opportunities for ecclesial service open to both men and women, according to their skills: and today's ecclesia should follow this pattern of broadly-based involvement and contribution from both brothers and sisters. As far as possible we should be looking to make these opportunities available. And there are many of them:

- Raising and guiding children (2 Timothy 1:5; 3:14-17; Titus 2:3-5)
- Prayer (1 Timothy 5:3-10)
- Arranging camps, conferences and special weekends
- Assisting with instruction and baptism
- Teaching sisters and the unbaptized, whether children at Sunday School or adults preparing for baptism (Acts 18:26; Titus 2:3-5)
- Greeting visitors to ecclesial meetings
- Providing pastoral care and counselling to the needy, the sick and the struggling
- Providing practical, personal care (Luke 8:1-3; John 12:3; 1 Timothy 5:3-10)
- Running facilities such as schools, hospitals and aged care facilities
- Providing hospitality for the ecclesia and its members (John 12:2; Acts 12:12; 16:15; Romans 16:3-15; Colossians 4:15)
- Distributing welfare (Acts 6; 9:36,39)
- Administering Sunday Schools

- Administering ecclesial finances and records
- Administering ecclesial libraries
- Supporting ecclesial worship by the playing of musical instruments
- Preaching by personal testimony, by correspondence or in mission areas (Luke 2:36-38; John 4:28-30; Matthew 28:5-10)
- Corresponding with those in isolation
- Contributing to the literature of God's family by writing and assisting with publication
- Speaking at events such as sisters' class, where the formal public teaching of men is not an issue (Luke 1:41-45; Acts 2:17,18; 21:9)

The list is in no particular order; and it is not exhaustive. Ecclesias will make arrangements according to their own needs in line with these principles.

Perhaps we need to stress that service is about our devotion to Christ, and to each other. It is there to meet the needs of others, not our own needs. Two apostolic exhortations remind us of the 'other' orientation of all service:

"Let each of us please his neighbour for his good, to build him up." (Romans 15:2)

"As each has received a gift, use it to serve one another, as good stewards of God's varied grace: whoever speaks, as one who speaks oracles of God; whoever serves, as one who serves by the strength that God supplies – in order that in everything God may be glorified through Jesus Christ. To him belong glory and dominion forever and ever. Amen." (1 Peter 4:10,11)

The head covering today

And what of Paul's instructions about the uncovering and the covering of the head in worship? Should they be adhered to strictly every time the Bible is opened, every time a prayer is offered or a hymn sung, or only when

135

the ecclesia is gathered in formal worship? If the practice is respected at formal ecclesial meetings, then surely conscience can decide its application in other circumstances.

Should we prescribe a certain form of covering, or demand a comprehensive covering? Paul calls for a head covering, not a hair covering, and his language is no more specific than that. Sincere implementation of this symbolism is enough. It will not be helpful to complicate obedience by multiplying human traditions.

Should the head covering be a spiritual statement, an understated scarf or veil, or should it be the kind of fashion statement that Peter and Paul actively discouraged? The answer is more obvious. Again, however, the Christ-likeness developing in the individual believer will guide the conscience, and we need not be too prescriptive about specific situations.

Our community rightly glories in the freedom of conscience for which the apostle fought so hard: but let every brother and sister acknowledge that the things Paul has written are "the commandments of the Lord", and honour him, and his Lord, by wholeheartedly embracing God's arrangements in spirit and truth.

In the ecclesia and in the home

Similar principles apply outside the ecclesial setting, in the home (1 Corinthians 7; Ephesians 5:21-33; Colossians 3:18,19; 1 Thessalonians 4:1-5; Titus 2:4,5; 1 Peter 3:1-7). Wives should submit themselves to their husbands, even when they are unbelievers. Husbands should love their wives in a self-giving way, and relate to them with self-control, respect and affection.

But we are not men and woman by virtue of marriage. Those who are single by choice or circumstance also have an important contribution to make. There are many Scriptural examples of single servants of God, both male and female: the greatest of all being the Servant, the Lord Jesus. Married or unmarried, we relate as men and women, and our complementary gifts glorify God when we work together as He intended us to do.

It will be important for the ecclesia to ensure that all members understand and support God's express purpose for men and women in the ecclesia and in the home. This can happen though structured teaching in Bible Class, Sunday School and Youth Group, and the provision of healthy role models and wise counsel to support loving, respectful relationships and fruitful marriages.

24

HE WHO HAS THE BRIDE IS
THE BRIDEGROOM

THIS is a great secret, Paul had said, with reference to marriage: "but I speak concerning Christ and the ecclesia." It is not at all surprising that one who was crucified with Christ, yet lived, yet knew no life but Christ living in him; who saw the developing spiritual life as "Christ in you, the hope of glory"; for whom to live was Christ, and to die was gain, because it catapulted him through time into the presence of his beloved Master – it is not at all surprising that "such a man" thought always of men and women and their relationships, as he thought about everything, in Christ-centred ways.

The ecclesia at Corinth, for example, was "a chaste virgin" espoused to Christ by Paul; and he worried jealously over her purity, lest she be seduced from the Jesus he had preached and the spirit he had imbued in her and the gospel which he had given her by those who claimed to be the messengers of Christ, but were not (2 Corinthians 11:1-4).

The figure draws on a lovely seam of New and Old Testament imagery. Before Paul, John the Baptist had seen himself as the friend of the bridegroom, destined to bring the bride to the wedding festivities then melt into the shadows, so that the lovers should have no lingering loyalty to any man, but think only of each other; so that disciples should not cling to John, but move on to the Lord Jesus without so much as a backward glance at the great man who had brought them to him (John 3:29,30). And before John, Isaiah had sung of the time when the righteousness of Jerusalem, and her salvation, should fill the earth with light, and God should finally rejoice over her with unmingled, unreserved, uncontained joy, "as the bridegroom rejoices over the bride" (Isaiah 62:5).

And beyond Paul, another John documented the extraordinary things he could see through the "door in heaven". "Let us rejoice and exult", thundered the voice of the great multitude, "for the marriage of the Lamb has come, and his Bride has made herself ready" (Revelation 19:7-9, cp. 21:2). Blessed indeed are "those who are invited to the marriage supper of the Lamb" (19:8), for we see something of the light and love and glad laughter of that time, and we long to be there, revelling in the company of Jesus Christ the King, revelling in the eternal life of God Himself.

Let us, above and before all things, give attention to hear him and do his will, that we may be ready to meet him when he comes. And may that same ready spirit be evident in our attitude to one another, and to his service, while we wait for this.

IN THE IMAGE OF GOD

SCRIPTURE INDEX

141

142

IN THE IMAGE OF GOD